THE I

THE PLAYMAKING WAY

Using Dramatic Arts to Support Young Readers and Writers

Rabin Nickens, M.S.Ed.

Third Power Publishing
New York

ISBN 13: 978-0-982110-2-7 (paperback)
ISBN 10: 0-9821100-2-2 (paperback)

Library of Congress Control Number: 2009901871

Third Power Publishing
P.O. Box 715
New York, NY 10037

www.RabinNickens.blogspot.com

Cover Designer: Junnita Jackson/ J3 Designs

Printed in the United States of America

To
Muriel Y. Nickens
The greatest teacher I have ever known.

ACKNOWLEDGMENTS

By far, the biggest influence on my life as an educator is the one to whom this book is dedicated, my mother, the poet Muriel Y. Nickens. Long before I became familiar with various educational theories and formal practices, she was my prime example of what good teaching should be. Things she did that I took for granted as a child – such as reading the Sunday comics with me; chatting with me about my day every time she came home from work and really listening; posting words all around the house so that my little sister could learn to read; allowing her children the freedom to speak their mind even if their opinions differed greatly from her own – I now realize were not only expressions of her love and interest, but also showed how education could be seamlessly woven into the fabric of a child's everyday life outside of school. Although she did not live to see the publication of this book, her respect and care for children is at its heart.

If my mother was the "principal" in our household, then my elder siblings were certainly her trusted deans, with their tutelage coming in many forms. Louis taught me that the city could be a classroom as he took me on what seemed like marathon-long urban nature hikes and visits to New York's various museums and libraries. Soraya's insights on everything from Pushkin, to Latimer, to the global impact and innovation of indigenous peoples, put my formal education in a much needed cultural/historical context. As Yvonne raised her own family, she helped me to understand the challenges of being a busy parent and appreciate any contribution they could make to their child's academic life. Even my younger sister Ariel influenced my views on education, as I observed how the mind of a gifted child like her had to be constantly stimulated and challenged in order to maintain interest and focus in school.

However, of all the deans, I must give special acknowledgment to my sister Louise. There would be no "Rabin the actress" or "Rabin the educator" without her. Some of my earliest memories are of watching her perform on stage and knowing in my heart that I wanted to do that, too. She would go on to help me realize my dream by enrolling me in various arts programs and personally coaching me for auditions and productions. As I began to use my talents to help other young people find their voice, Louise became the first one to tell me "You are a natural-born teacher." Although I resisted this designation for many years, she finally helped me see how I could synergize my identity as a performing artist with life as an educator in a way that was fulfilling for both me and the thousands of students I would eventually serve. This was extremely challenging at times, but when the going got rough, she always had a way of convincing me to not give up, and helped me focus on what matters most – the children.

I would also like to acknowledge a number of wonderful friends and colleagues from the world of education, the arts, and everywhere in between, who have inspired me, influenced my practice, and helped make this book possible.

Lee (Mr. Lee) Peters: One of the most intuitive theatre directors I've had the pleasure of working with. Thank you for reading my drafts and providing feedback that was clear, honest, and candid.

Gabrielle (Ata-Gabby) Price: As I navigated through the drama that is the publishing industry, thanks for keeping me focused, and encouraging me to go out there and get things done.

Susan Herriott: Thank you for sharing such great publishing resources with me and steering me in the "write" direction.

Torica Webb: Fellow educator and awesome anthropologist, *kia ora* for lending an ear and reminding me that the well-being and nurturing of the teacher is crucial to the well-being of the student.

Vijay Nelson: A brilliant educator and colleague who truly respects and believes in the capabilities of children. Thanks for your early feedback on my manuscript, and for being one of the teachers who "test-drove" my methods in your own classroom.

Kim (Miss Kim) Kaufmann: A great teaching assistant and friend. Thanks for your time and energy, and demonstrating approaches that always allowed for children to be children. "Good job, good job!"

Cheryl Lynn Hendrickson: A model of creative independence. Thank you for taking me under your wing early on and inspiring me to strike out on my own, my way.

Debra Hopkins and Mark Dempsey: As mentors and friends you were part of my growth from outspoken teen advocating for my peers, to grown woman using my experiences to continue that advocacy through education. Thanks for your years of advice, care, and commitment to youth empowerment.

Dr. Donna M. Jones: Thank you for your mentorship, making my Bank Street College experience possible, and encouraging me to share my knowledge with the rest of the world. Your dedication to effecting positive change for children and educators still inspires me.

Bank Street College of Education: Thank you for shaping my view that education should conform to the nature and needs of the child and not the other way around. As a proud alumna and lifelong learner I am particularly grateful for access to the treasure trove that is the Bank Street College library and its helpful staff.

To my students, particularly those in the village of Harlem, the most brilliant and resilient individuals I know: Meeting the challenge of teaching you all these years brought out a creativity and strength I never knew I had. It has been an honor to be of service to you, your families, and your communities.

CONTENTS

ABOUT THE AUTHOR

Rabin Nickens is a dynamic New York City-based educator with over 15 years of experience as a classroom teacher, dramatic arts instructor, performing artist, and advocate for children. In her mission to "help young people empower themselves through education and the arts," she has worked with thousands of kindergarten through 12th grade children of diverse backgrounds, helping them discover the talents and aptitudes within them.

Rabin earned her Master of Science degree in early childhood and elementary education from Bank Street College. Her theatre training includes study at Baruch College, Black Spectrum Theatre, Joy of Performing Theatre Ensemble, and the New Federal Theatre Workshops where she worked with master thespians such as Ruby Dee and Dr. Barbara Ann Teer. Her advocacy work began with appointment to the Mayor's Youth Advisory Council, where she advised former New York City mayor David N. Dinkins and other high-ranking city officials on issues affecting youth. She went on to recruit and lead other teams of youth who were awarded the Brooklyn District Attorney's Peace Keeper Award for non-violent community action.

She is the recipient of numerous honors including the Friars Foundation Scholarship for Excellence in Theatre Arts, a curriculum-writing grant from Columbia University's Teachers College, and the Theodore Roosevelt Association Medal for Public Speaking. When she is not in the classroom, Rabin travels internationally studying world cultures, and conducts professional development trainings and presentations on topics in education and cross-cultural competency for organizations such as The National Association for the Education of Young Children (NAEYC), Kappa Delta Pi International Honor Society in Education, NAFSA: Association of International Educators, and The Student Conservation Association (SCA).

PREFACE

In the course of my work in culturally, linguistically, and economically diverse communities as both a classroom teacher and dramatic arts instructor, I have been consistently impressed by how much children of all ages and backgrounds can excel with the right combination of guidance and support. However, I have also been struck by the number of students, particularly those in the early childhood and elementary grades, who still had difficulty fully grasping language arts concepts and skills. For example, although writing with consistently correct spelling, punctuation, and grammar is a praise-worthy accomplishment, mechanics are not the only things that make strong writers. Depending on the genre, writers must also know how to properly organize their ideas, focus those ideas, and then elaborate on them—all of which can be hard for young children to execute on paper.

Furthermore, I encountered many students who were able to read smoothly, pronouncing words and phrases with few or no errors, and even with some level of expression. Yet when asked questions about the text, they did not always seem to "get it" on a deeper level. This is because reading is more than decoding words and having fluency. Children must also understand what they read, which actually involves thinking as they read. Thinking skills that adults often take for granted—such as finding the main idea and important details of a text, making inferences, and distinguishing the different parts of a story—can be a huge struggle for young readers. As they get older and the assigned text becomes more complex, so does the type of thinking involved in comprehending it. These challenges often result in students becoming frustrated and sometimes losing interest in reading and writing altogether.

Some of the problem is because the very language arts skills we want children to master are abstract. Whereas in the area of mathematics, there are "manipulatives" (such as geoboards, pattern blocks, counters, and cubes) for students to touch, move, and explore with in order to help make abstract numerical concepts concrete, I realized that there were really no such manipulatives for language arts.

The challenge can be even greater for English language learners and new immigrants, who not only struggle with language acquisition but also must build background knowledge in order to understand the new cultural context of the material they are reading.

In addition, when schools put their emphasis on struggling students, those children who are already performing at grade level or higher can be left feeling neglected and bored. There is also a level of frustration for teachers of highly diverse and inclusive classrooms, who may find it difficult to engage and challenge their "gifted and talented" students while also adequately tending to the needs of other students. In fact, I was once one of those teachers.

I developed *The Playmaking Way*, a dramatic arts and literacy enrichment methodology, to address all of these challenges. Utilizing my background as an actress, I was able to make a remarkable observation early on—that the thinking and activities involved in making a play are closely related to the thinking and skills children must master in order to become exceptional readers, writers, and speakers. I was amazed by how much of what I was asking my students to do in terms of analyzing a text and creating a story was reminiscent of the interactions between actors and directors when bringing a story to life on stage.

Playmaking can provide educators with a way to enhance their students' literacy skills and meet both language arts and dramatic arts standards, through multisensory, experiential activities that help students gain a new perspective on abstract concepts they may not grasp through other means. In this way, playmaking not only fosters students' creative development but also acts as that missing language-arts manipulative.

As students have fun creating and enacting plays, attending dramatic performances, and designing sets, they also explore themes and issues that are of interest to them. This in turn helps them build the background knowledge and vocabulary necessary to excel in their reading and writing studies, as well as other subjects outside their playmaking projects.

The Playmaking Way is a guide for educators of young children, whether classroom teachers, dramatic arts instructors, or community theatre directors. The primary goals are to help educators use playmaking as follows:

♦ to integrate dramatic arts into early-childhood and elementary curriculums (kindergarten through third grade) in a practical yet child-centered way, and

♦ to enhance their students' language arts skills and social development.

This book details how the playmaking process works, step by step. As a case study throughout, I refer to the process of making a play entitled *Family Drama* in collaboration with children in a first-grade class I taught in Harlem, New York City. We worked together to plan, write, set-design, and perform the play, based on the theme of family relationships. The content came from the students' own experiences, discussions, field trips, and readings on the subject. While my experiences with these and other early-childhood and elementary-aged students forms the primary basis for this guide, I include a solid theoretical foundation for my practices as well. I have also cited several scholarly works that offer alternatives to my approach and will give educators many opportunities to integrate drama in a way that suits their unique needs, teaching styles, and context.

Although various texts on the topic of drama in education can be quite informative, they often focus on acting technique or overemphasize a finished product. This guide, however, is more concerned with the development of the whole child through the process of dramatic arts, not necessarily with producing an award-winning performance.

In addition, many texts discuss drama in education without considering the challenges of different educational environments, including limited time and resources, classroom management issues, and the pressure to have students meet state educational standards. Furthermore, many teachers are unable to explore dramatic arts in their classrooms because their school district, administration, or even parents do not see the direct educational value in it. This guide was created with these challenges in mind, and it contains information and strategies that busy teachers can use to make the integration of dramatic arts in the classroom more feasible.

This guide is also designed to be straightforward and to the point. It synthesizes extensive research in education and dramatic arts into a form that is actually practical to use. However, I highly recommend that you review the cited materials whenever you can if you are interested in an in-depth understanding of the theoretical grounding of my techniques.

HOW TO USE THIS GUIDE

This guide is divided into four main parts:

Part 1: "An Introduction to Playmaking" gives an overview of the playmaking process, how it works, and why it works. You will find much of the theoretical foundation behind this methodology here.

Part 2: "Getting Started" suggests all the materials you will need, how to plan in advance, and other issues to consider before starting playmaking with your students.

Part 3: "The Playmaking Process" could be considered the "nitty-gritty." This section describes the details of the process step by step, from students sharing their experiences to the performance of a student-written theatrical production.

Part 4: "Follow-Up and Assessment" suggests ways to check student progress and understanding throughout the playmaking project. Assessment should be considered before you embark on a playmaking project, but this section is placed toward the end of the book so you first familiarize yourself with the activities involved in playmaking and how you can use them to learn more about your students. Some teachers may want to skip ahead to this section and then come back to it again after reading the rest of the book.

In addition, the "**Reference**" section offers a good way to expand your knowledge about dramatic arts and constructivist education. Within the "**Appendices**," you will find materials that complement and illustrate key parts of the playmaking process and act as tools to support your work in the classroom.

Please note that the process of playmaking does not have to strictly follow the linear order indicated in the table of contents. The topics are listed this way simply so you can find information quickly. As you will see, activities such as scriptwriting and set design are interrelated and thus can be done simultaneously.

PART 1:
AN INTRODUCTION TO PLAYMAKING

1.1 WHAT IS PLAYMAKING?

Simply put, playmaking is a way to help students write, produce, and perform plays that they create together as a class. However, to better understand what makes playmaking unique, one should consider how plays are usually done. Traditionally, the process of theatre production goes as follows:

♦ A director and/or producer selects a ready-made script of a play they want performed.

♦ They then hold auditions to cast the actors who will perform the play.

♦ During this time they may also hire set designers to build scenery for the play.

♦ The actors memorize the words exactly as written in the script.

♦ Next, they conduct rehearsals with the actors over the course of several days or weeks.

♦ Finally, the play is performed in front of an audience of the general public.

In this example, the process of script selection, casting, set design, and rehearsal are all means to an end—a play that entertains an audience. It involves people acting out plays that someone else has written. Usually when plays are done in the classroom, this means students are acting out plays an adult has written.

Playmaking differs in that the goal is not just the satisfaction of an audience (although that can be a positive result); instead, the goal is the growth and development of the child through making the play. In other words, the making of a play is not a means to an end, but the end in and of itself. Since the goal of playmaking is different from traditional theatre productions, the process also differs in the following ways:

- ◆ A teacher helps select a theme for the play based on student interests and needs.
- ◆ Students explore this theme through a variety of guided activities.
- ◆ Students create stories to enact based on discoveries made during exploration.
- ◆ Next, the teacher helps students work cooperatively to act out these stories through improvisation.
- ◆ Students create dialogue and any necessary props or scenery as they go along.
- ◆ The teacher transcribes the dialogue the students create and puts it in the form of a script.
- ◆ Students take on roles and responsibilities, whether as actors, set designers, etc., based on teacher assessment of students' strengths, needs, and wants.
- ◆ Students rehearse by continuing to replay the stories, with the script acting as a guideline.
- ◆ Finally, a play or series of skits is performed in front of an audience of parents and other classes.

In playmaking, students are guided through the story rather than expected to master acting technique. They work cooperatively rather than featured as individuals. Students act out and improvise stories they create as opposed to dramatizing children's books someone else has written. They keep replaying their improvisations for the purpose of deeper understanding and internalization of the theme they are acting out, not necessarily to master word-for-word memorization of text. The performance of the play simply acts as the culminating activity, similar to any other activity at the end of a unit of study. This method often creates a comfort level for students that may alleviate the competitiveness and anxiety associated with traditional theatre productions.

1.2 WHAT ARE THE LEARNING OBJECTIVES OF PLAYMAKING?

Early childhood and elementary classrooms can gain much from the experience of integrating drama into the curriculum. The playmaking process in particular is an educational experience not only for the students, but for the teacher as well. It puts the students in the empowering role of storytellers, communicating what they know and what they learn in an organized yet creative way. During the process, students will develop:

◆ creativity and aesthetic skills
◆ critical thinking skills
◆ social growth and the ability to work cooperatively with others
◆ a sense of spatial relationships
◆ fine and gross motor skills
◆ improved oral communication skills
◆ enhanced reading comprehension and writing skills

As the teacher, you will not only enhance your students' learning but also have the satisfaction of:

◆ addressing the needs of diverse learners
◆ helping students meet state and national learning standards
◆ exploring issues relevant to your students' lives
◆ making learning fun for your students.

1.3 WHY INTEGRATE PLAYMAKING INTO THE CURRICULUM?

1. Playmaking Builds Off Of Children's Prior Knowledge

According to theorist and pioneer of progressive education John Dewey, the quality of a child's development depends on, among other things, the quality of the activities the child experiences. Educators should ensure that each experience "both takes up something from those which have gone before and modifies in some way the qualities of those that come after" (Dewey, 1938, p. 35). The activities involved with playmaking meet Dewey's criteria in that they build off of the personal experiences, problem-solving skills, and language-arts skills children already have in order to further develop these competencies and enable children to deal with more complex real-life experiences in the future.

2. Playmaking Is Child-Centered Education

Dewey (1938) also explained that an experience is only educational if its planning, the subject matter, and related teaching tools are connected with consideration for students' abilities and interests.

To support these ideas, Dewey presented the example of "traditional" education, wherein teachers chose certain subject matter and materials under the pretense that they were justified simply because the activities worked with other students in the past. They did so without taking into consideration the effects on the unique individuals currently being taught. It was a "one-size-fits-all" attitude toward curriculum that unfortunately still exists today. The only students who learned were those for whom the material just happened to be well suited, while everyone else simply had to manage or not learn at all. He stated that "failure of adaptation of material to needs and capacities of individuals may cause an experience to be non-educative" (Dewey, 1938, 46). In other words, it is not only the job of the student to adapt to curriculum, but teachers must try to adapt the curriculum to suit the student's needs in order for the experience to be truly educational.

The playmaking process described in this guide does just that. It is designed to begin with exploration of a theme the students are interested in, not just the teacher. It keeps students engaged by providing a variety of responsibilities and roles to play, on and off the stage, that you the teacher can modify to meet the unique needs, experiences, and skill sets of your students. Everyone will feel they can succeed in some way, because everyone can participate.

3. Playmaking Helps Children With Diverse Learning Styles Learn

Noted psychologist Howard Gardner's theory of multiple intelligences reinforces the notion that studying the arts reaches some children in ways that other instruction may not (Rasmussen, 1998). How many times have teachers had those one or two (or more) students who "just don't get it" no matter how many times a particular concept is taught to them using the standard curriculum? This often causes frustration and low morale for both the student and teacher, who are no doubt working hard toward the child's success. Also consider that, often, the average curriculum involves long periods when children have to be quiet and listen to mini lectures and then perhaps complete workbook pages. Some children might be able to learn through this more linguistic approach, but what about those students who tend to process information in a different way?

Playmaking gives teachers an alternative and effective way reach those children, because the playmaking process is multisensory in nature, providing many activities that embody several learning modalities at the same time. Children will benefit from playmaking whether they respond best to moving and talking or prefer to sit quietly and listen. There is flexibility inherent in playmaking activities so that every child can learn in his or her own unique way. Indeed, "the arts offer an expanded notion of classroom discourse that is not solely grounded in linear, objective language and thinking, but rather recognizes the full range of human potential for expression and understanding" (Gallas, 1991, p. 42).

4. *Playmaking Supports Language Arts Learning*

Playmaking is not meant to replace your existing language arts instruction; it complements it. The activities involved in playmaking can help your students make their own meaning of the language arts concepts you teach. These activities actively engage the students in thinking about stories as they create and act them out. As the children plan, analyze, and modify their performances, they get to practice strategies that mirror drafting and revision strategies used to improve writing. In the process of reviewing and discussing performances, students are practicing the same type of strategies, such as inferring and questioning, that will aid their reading comprehension.

5. *Playmaking Develops Skills Relevant To Other Content Areas*

Through participation in activities like those in playmaking, students expand upon and develop capacities for critical thinking and problem solving (Rasmussen, 1998), skills that will aid them in other subject areas, such as science and mathematics. In fact, research done by Robert S. Root-Bernstein (1997), professor of physiology at Michigan State University, indicates "that active participation and demonstrated ability in one or more of the arts are far more predicative of success in science than standard measures such as nQ., scores on tests such as the SAT, or academic degrees" (p. B6). For example, through playmaking, students consider spatial relationships as they design sets. A sense of spatial relationship is also important in mathematics. As students formulate ideas about the traits of characters they see performed or that they perform themselves, they are also practicing the same type of inferential thinking necessary to achieve higher levels of reading comprehension.

It should be noted that there is some controversy among arts educators about whether the arts should be integrated into the curriculum to support academic achievement in other content areas, or if the arts should be taught for art's sake, regardless of how or if it relates to other content areas. I prefer to take a dialectical approach to playmaking, because I believe that both positions are interconnected. As Paul Lehman, professor emeritus in the school of music at the University of Michigan states, "These are not mutually exclusive ideas. Human activity is inherently interdisciplinary. We don't divide up our day into disciplinary parts" (Rasmussen, 1998). Thus, we do not always have to divide up our curriculum into discrete parts, either. Playmaking offers the chance to explore several content areas and allows education to take place in a more holistic way.

6. Playmaking Is Developmentally Appropriate

Playmaking is adaptable to children of all ages, yet some educators may be skeptical about the ability of very young children to engage in this type of learning in a coordinated way. However, they may be surprised to find that playmaking is actually grounded in the nature and needs of children in the early childhood grades, ages five to nine in particular. At these stages in their development, children love to ask questions, explain things, work with their hands, learn new games, and participate in cooperative play (Wood, 2007). Playmaking allows children to learn by utilizing and expanding upon these natural tendencies.

Playmaking is also appropriate for the range of developmental tendencies in highly diverse early childhood classrooms. Around the age of six or seven, to varying degrees, children "can perform tasks independently, formulate goals, and resist the temptation to abandon them" (Cole, Cole, & Lightfoot, 2005, p. 451). From a biological standpoint, agility, balance, and coordination all improve significantly during this period. In terms of comprehension, noted educator and researcher Robbie Case (1998) suggests that increases in memory allow children to consider two or more aspects of a problem at one time. The increased duration and complexity of children's play during this period in their lives seems to indicate they are capable of regulating their own behavior according to agreed-upon social rules (Cole et al., 2005). According to educational theorist Jean Piaget (1932/1965), while children's thinking about social rules is initially based on respect for authority, it eventually becomes based on mutual respect and consent. Ultimately, children become able to govern themselves. So, contrary to what some believe are the limitations of working with this age group, it stands to reason that with the proper guidance, children at this stage of development have the mental and physical capacity to work cooperatively on multiple tasks and activities, such as those involved with playmaking.

On the other hand, these same children may be at a stage of cognitive development in which they are unable to understand other people's perspective and thought processes and to reason about cause and effect, or to distinguish appearance from reality. Through participation in the playmaking process, particularly when they perform and analyze character traits and motives, children get a chance to develop those skills. Note that these types of skills are of tremendous use when it comes to meeting learning standards in reading comprehension and the craft of writing. Those of you who have administered standardized tests to your students know that reasoning about cause and effect, distinguishing between the genres of fiction and nonfiction, and understanding the perspective of characters are all abilities children are expected to have to varying degrees.

7. Playmaking Helps Develop Abstract Thinking Skills

According to Maxine Greene, philosopher-in-residence at the Lincoln Center Institute, art stimulates the imagination in a unique way (Greene, 2001). Imagination is essential in education because it gives human beings the ability to "enter a created world, an invented world ... to find new perspectives opening on our lived worlds" (Greene, 2001, p. 82).

For many young people, reading a short story, chapter book, or poem is like entering one of those "created" worlds, seeming quite abstract, far from their own experience and immediate understanding. Playmaking gives students the unique opportunity to use their imagination to enter worlds of their own creation. Their stories and those of their peers come to life and take on new dimensions as they embody characters that they have developed. In the process, they analyze characters, settings, and themes in such a way that they transform their imagination into a tool they can use to make sense of abstraction in their reading and other areas of their lives outside of the classroom.

PART 2:

GETTING STARTED

So you have decided to embark on a creative journey with your students, one that will result in a theatrical production you will all be proud of. You may have already discussed the idea of making a play with your students, and now everyone (including you) is excited and eager to start. However, before you begin you will need to consider the following to ensure the playmaking process is successful.

2.1 MATERIALS

Very few materials are needed for playmaking other than what teachers probably already have in the classroom. The scope of materials can be as basic or as elaborate as your resources allow. However, some teachers find it helpful to gather and set aside materials their students will use specifically for playmaking in the form of a "prop box." This could be an actual box, crate, basket, bin, shelf, or closet filled with items students can use as costumes or props when they act out characters and want to replicate the settings for their stories. Here are some suggestions:

PLAYMAKING PROP BOX	
fabric	paper towel tubes
sheets	sheets
paper or plastic plates	construction paper
plastic cups	tape
cardboard boxes (empty shoeboxes, cereal boxes, file boxes, etc.)	hats
	rope
	aluminum foil

I suggest that you take a survey of your classroom first to see what you already have. With some imagination, desks can turn into fast food counters, chairs can turn into cars, and a child's sweater can turn into a superhero's cape. Be creative! If you still feel the need for additional materials, save money by going to thrift shops or garage sales. You could also ask parents for items to borrow or donate. Remember, using items that can be recycled and transformed into props or scenery is one way to practice environmental conservation and to explore this concept with your students.

Some teachers may find it helpful to also have a video camera to record parts of the improvisation and rehearsal phase.

Reviewing the videotape with the whole class offers another way to reflect on the action and dialogue performed. The video also comes in handy when working with the class to transcribe selected dialogue into a script. Reading the "Acting Out" and "Scripting" sections of this guide will help you decide whether you want to use video in this way. Do not forget to obtain permission from your school's administration and parents if you choose to videotape.

2.2 CLASSROOM ENVIRONMENT

There should be a clear, open space in your classroom for at least three or four students to move around and act out stories. This will act as the "stage" area in your classroom. It is certainly not necessary to take your students to a huge school auditorium, especially since doing so can be very intimidating for young children. The exception, of course, is if your students want to use the auditorium and you actually have one at your disposal on a regular basis. As an early childhood teacher, you probably already have an area that you use for group instruction, block building, or to gather children around for storytelling. This should be sufficient to do double-duty as a playmaking area. You can also teach your children how to make space in the classroom for playmaking time by moving a few desks or chairs. See the appendix for a diagram of one of my classroom setups.

2.3 TIMEFRAME/PACING

Playmaking projects run similarly to a thematic unit of study that culminates in a final project—the play. However, the timeframe in which you want to complete a particular playmaking project is up to you. The pacing is flexible in that you can decide how much time you want to take to complete each phase of the process. You may want to consider your daily class schedule, how much time is allotted for each period in your school's day, and whether it's standardized testing time. With this in mind, a play production could be accomplished in as little as four weeks or take as long as eight weeks. Note that due to the nature of playmaking, many of the activities overlap. For example, although "Scripting" is its own section in this guide, you will find that much of the script develops while you are in the "Acting Out" phase. Therefore, any pacing calendar you create should act as a general framework with the assumption that some flexibility will be inherent in it. See the Appendix for a sample pacing calendar based on a six-week playmaking unit that I conducted during the springtime.

Another factor in how long a playmaking project can take is how you integrate its activities into your daily scheduled curriculum. If, for example, you see this project primarily as a way to learn about drama, then you might decide to devote a period each day or a couple of times a week solely to this project. For some schools, this might be done during your "extended time," "choice period," or "activity center" time. In this case, your daily schedule might look something like this:

SAMPLE DAILY SCHEDULE – A	
Period	**Subject**
1	PHONICS
2	READING
3	WRITING
4	PREP
5	LUNCH
6	MATH
7	SCIENCE
8	EXTENDED TIME (Playmaking)
9	DISMISSAL

On the other hand, if you see this project primarily as a way for students to learn *through* the drama—in other words, learning about reading comprehension skills—then you might schedule playmaking activities during your literacy period. In that case, your schedule might look like this:

SAMPLE DAILY SCHEDULE – B	
Period	**Subject**
1	PHONICS
2	READING
3	WRITING (Playmaking)
4	PREP
5	LUNCH
6	READ ALOUD (Playmaking)
7	MATH
8	SCIENCE
9	DISMISSAL

In the above schedule, rather than separate playmaking out, it is incorporated into another related subject area's time. Personal narratives that students work on during your writing period may turn into skits to be acted out later in the playmaking process. During your "Read Aloud" time, you may choose a book that relates to the theme of the play your students want to perform. As you can probably already tell, of all the typical subject areas, playmaking activities most directly relate to language arts, which is why it is a bit easier to incorporate playmaking during these periods in the day. By using an interdisciplinary approach, your students may work on their playmaking project during your regular day and still accomplish the learning objectives associated with other content areas at the same time.

2.4 PARENT PARTICIPATION

Parents and caregivers can be involved throughout the playmaking process through visits to the classroom to share family stories, do read alouds, and share their own artistic skills. They can also accompany the class on field trips. Parents and other family members can provide recognition for the children by attending the culminating dramatic performance. According to professor Susan M. Swap (1993), "knowing that an audience is coming to review or witness one's work adds energy, motivation … as well as more meaning to the outcome" (p. 129).

For parents with impaired mobility, there are ways to contribute from home. For example, they can lend items to use for props or send homemade arts, crafts, or CDs of music. However, when possible, provisions should be made to accommodate these parents' needs by making them aware of the school's wheelchair-accessible entrances and providing space for mobility devices in the classroom and performance areas.

A sample "Parent Participation Letter" in the Appendix can be used to help determine how parents are willing and able to participate. However, despite your best efforts and intentions as a teacher, some parents may find it difficult to become involved for several reasons, including time constraints, personal problems, or feelings of intimidation or mistrust when dealing with educators and school staff members (Rockwell, Andre, & Hawley, 1996). Cultural differences or language barriers may also hinder communication and participation.

To address these challenges, it might be advantageous to invite parents to a conveniently scheduled open house. At this meeting, you could do a simple presentation about the project, explaining how it benefits families and enhances student learning, and listing, step by step, ways that parents can be involved. You can also ask parents their opinions. Parents would have their concerns addressed through a question-and-answer period and could schedule time to participate in specific playmaking activities with you either verbally or by using the Parent Participation Letter mentioned above. Ask your school administrators if it is okay to hold a general meeting at the school in the evening. Sometimes, I conducted meetings during my prep periods for parents who worked nights and were only available during the day.

In the case of parents of English language learners, you might invite them to a meeting where you provide an adult translator. If the school is not able to provide a professional translator, you may invite a multilingual colleague or a language student from a local university. It is preferable not to use children as translators, because it may put them under tremendous pressure and may place them in a status position that is inappropriate in the family's culture (Swap, 1993).

No matter what the level of participation, parents should be recognized for their contributions. I sometimes did this by writing brief notes about them in our class's weekly newsletter. Recognition like this helps parents "feel valued and supported, and often renews interest in continuing to contribute" (Swap, 1993, p. 127).

2.5 CLASSROOM MANAGEMENT: "THE FIVE Ps" MAXIM

A principal once shared a saying with me: "Proper Preparation Prevents Poor Performance." Although I do not know that she was referring directly to classroom management, per se, I believe this maxim still applies. If your goals, pacing, and materials are well thought out in advance, and you have done your best to seek out parent support, many potential classroom management problems will be prevented.

In addition, some classroom management and discipline issues can be addressed by reinforcing the concepts of roles, routines, and responsibilities, which you probably already established at the beginning of the year. It helps when those roles include assigning "transition monitors" responsible for helping set up materials at the start of given activities, and also cleaning up or reorganizing the room at the end. Positive reinforcement, such as praise for students' active involvement and teamwork, is also a great influence. In my experience, most children are so interested in participating in this type of experiential learning that they are motivated to behave respectfully and cooperatively so they can get to do these activities over and over again.

PART 3:

THE PLAYMAKING PROCESS

Exploring a Theme

Creating Stories

Acting Out

Set Design, Props, and Costumes

Scripting

Casting

Rehearsal

Performance

3.1 EXPLORING A THEME

> *"A narrative with action and people but without theme is a story without meaning that leaves the reader wondering at the close, 'So what?'"* — Rebecca J. Lukens (2003), educator

The above statement about literature by noted educator and author Rebecca J. Lukens also holds true for performance. By helping students consider and choose a theme or topic for their playmaking unit, you are starting them on the road to higher-order thinking beyond just recall of facts, and moving them toward deeper meanings and lessons about human nature, whether in the stories they read and hear or the ones they will create. You are helping them elevate the stories they create to the level of literature, as opposed to simply stories with beginnings and endings.

As an educator, you must help students choose a theme for their play that is based on their own needs and interests. You might discover potential themes by seeing commonalities in the subjects of your students' journal writing, by observing the way they interact in the schoolyard or at recess, or by listening in on their conversations at lunchtime. For example, through discussions with some of my first-grade students, I found out that they loved their families but were also concerned about varying degrees of conflict in their home life. At that stage in their development, children have a need to share, especially about their family. "Family" is also considered an appropriate topic in many first-grade social studies curriculums. Consequently, we chose to base our play on the theme of family, and more specifically, how they resolve conflicts. Some teachers will encourage their students to choose a theme that relates to a social issue in their school or community, or a current topic from the social studies curriculum. The choice is up to you and your students, but other suggestions for playmaking themes include the following:

PLAYMAKING THEMES/TOPICS		
friendship	communities working together	teacher/student relationships
bullying	conflict resolution	sharing
teamwork	sports	hobbies
going away	being new	visiting family
conquering fear	forgiveness	growing up
divorce	pollution/conservation	stereotypes

Next, after choosing a theme, you can engage in exploration activities. These primarily serve to deepen children's understanding of issues involved with the chosen theme, but also introduce students to concepts involved with the playmaking process. This could be considered "building background knowledge" in preparation for the dramatic arts work to come. In keeping with ideas put forth by educational theorist John Dewey (1938), it also helps students make their own meaning of the theme through experience. The goal is to have students become as familiar with and knowledgeable about the theme as possible, so that the ideas that come from this exploration will become the motivation and content for their performances later on. Although the whole playmaking process is an exploration of sorts, the "Exploring the Theme" section of this guide highlights those activities that do not involve dramatic performance.

There are a variety of ways to explore and learn more about your chosen theme, but I chose to explore the family conflict theme primarily through literacy activities (such as read alouds, journal writing, and storytelling) for a number of reasons. For starters, since playmaking is essentially a form of storytelling, it naturally has a connection with literacy. Reading, writing, listening, and speaking are also integral parts of dramatic arts. Furthermore, while these types of activities facilitated understanding of our dramatic arts theme, they simultaneously helped to meet many state and national standards for English language arts.

Another compelling reason to use these activities was that I was already using them during our literacy block. One of the great things about doing activities you are already familiar with from other content areas is that there are no techniques to learn from scratch. Time constraints become less of an issue, because the activities can be done during their usual content area block, rather than trying to squeeze in or create an additional period solely devoted to the purpose of this exploration (although if that's possible in your school and your daily schedule, by all means, do it). The following are brief descriptions of some literacy activities I have used with my students to explore our chosen themes. More details on these and other types of activities that enhance language arts learning can be found in *Classrooms That Work* (Cunningham & Allington, 2007) and *Reading & Writing in ESL* (Peregoy & Boyle, 2008). To find out more about the role of theme in children's literature, you may refer to Rebecca J. Lukens's *A Critical Handbook of Children's Literature* (2003).

Read Alouds

In playmaking, read alouds involve preparing a collection of books based on the theme of your play. In consultation with our literacy staff developer, I obtained grade-level literature related to family from our school library, and I was able to conduct a completely integrated course of study (see the Appendix for a sample bibliography of books used for our theme). You could also involve students in the selection process by encouraging them to visit the school or neighborhood library and borrow books related to your theme. In this way, you are motivating them to use the library as a resource and develop research skills, and in the case of the neighborhood library, you're helping them see the value of institutions in their very own community.

Although I read the selected books aloud to the whole class, I also made them available for independent reading time by putting them in a bin marked "family" in our classroom library. These thematic books were sometimes read in place of other text during the shared reading or guided reading time within the literacy block. At times, I would remind students to pay attention to the characters in the story, where the story took place, what the story was mainly about, and the order in which the events took place. These are the same things we have to consider when telling a story through a play. I introduced or reinforced terms such as "character," "setting," and even "conflict" at this time. The reading and post-discussions compelled students to think about how families in the story related to each other while comparing and contrasting with their own experiences. These activities also served as a motivation for journal writing later on.

During or after the reading, you may also ask questions that help children think about the feelings and the perspectives of others. For example, while reading *Big Mama and Grandma Ghana* by Angela Shelf Medearis, a book about a boy visited by both of his grandmothers, you might ask students, "Why do you think Grandma laughed?" at a certain point in the story, or "How do you think the boy felt when he played checkers with Big Mama?" The development of this kind of inferential thinking will also help students with the characterization involved in the improvisations to come in the playmaking process.

Storytelling

Storytelling involves giving students the opportunity to verbally share personal stories related to the theme. For my students, this was sometimes as simple as responding to questions during our morning meeting such as, "So what did you do with your family this weekend?" Sometimes it was a response to literature, where I asked them to make self-to-text connections by relating something we read to their own personal experience. For example, after reading *Big Mama and Grandma Ghana*, I asked different students, "Can you tell us about a time when one of your grandparents came to stay with you?" This type of sharing and discussion is valuable because it involves children creating a narrative form, which is not only an integral part of playmaking, but an opportunity to practice oral language skills as well.

All stories must have a beginning, middle, and end. Many children will provide detail of this type but, depending on where they are developmentally, they may start with simple responses such as, "My grandma came to stay with us last week." This is a teachable moment where you can encourage a child to expand her story through some strategic questioning. You might ask, "What did you do together?" or "What's the first thing you did when she first arrived?" Then you could ask, "What did you do after that?" Finally, you might ask, "What did you do just before she left?"

Note that the above are open-ended questions that deal with time and order of events. However, you can engage in other lines of questioning that reflect the type of reading comprehension required at this stage of their development. Using the simple nursery rhyme of "Jack and Jill," below are some examples of other types of questions you may ask students regarding stories they hear during storytelling or read alouds.

- ◆ sequence (*What happened before Jill came tumbling down the hill?*)
- ◆ inferences (*Why do you think they went to fetch the pail of water?*)
- ◆ main idea (*What was this story mostly about?*)
- ◆ setting (*Where did this story happen? What time of day?*)
- ◆ character traits (*Think about what Jack and Jill do in the story. What word would you use to describe someone who does things like that?*)
- ◆ cause and effects (*Why/how did Jack break his crown?*)
- ◆ details (*Who went up the hill?*)

◆   fact vs. opinions (*If I say Jack and Jill are silly, is that a fact or an opinion?*)

Of course, the exact wording of these questions would vary depending on the particulars of the story being told or read, as well as what your language arts learning goals are, the skill level of your students, and your own personal style. Again, this type of engagement not only prepares students for the type of reading comprehension questions children at this age level may be expected to answer (whether reading for pleasure or on standardized tests), but it will also help them better understand and bring to life characters they may play in later performances.

Journal Writing in Drama Books

My students also got to share their stories through writing. When we commenced this project, I helped my students make their own journals, or "drama books" as we called them, using lined writing paper stapled in between construction paper for covers. Students were allowed to decorate the book however they wanted to. I explained that this was a special place where they could write about experiences that really happened to them (personal narratives), but because this was a drama book, they should try to only write about experiences or topics related to our playmaking theme, family conflict. I also let students know that we might end up acting out their stories, if they wanted.

Your students' drama books could also be store-bought marble notebooks (I recommend this type because the pages are bound with string and less likely to fall out than spiral notebooks). The advantage of actually making a drama book is that you can create it with different types of writing paper, depending on the needs of your students. Either way, the books can be as simple or as detailed as you want.

Many children in my class became very attached to their drama books and wanted to write in them any chance they could get. These opportunities most often came as responses to literature, when they were allowed to free-write about their experiences, or answered the same type of questions they had responded to verbally during read-aloud or storytelling time. A field trip may spark a memory and inspire students to write it down. Sometimes drama book writing was part of a quiet morning activity after students arrived at school and put away their things. They could also write whatever was on their mind about the theme whenever they had free time or needed a release.

This activity is particularly helpful to children who are better writers than speakers or who might not be comfortable sharing verbally in a group. It also gives children more time to think about what they want to communicate and how. As I stated before, you may already do journal writing in your classroom in your own way. The only difference is that we continuously used the theme of family conflict as a prompt for writing in the drama books.

Since the purpose of this activity is to garner ideas that will be used later for improvisations, I was more concerned with the quality of the content than with perfect spelling or grammar in drama books. In some cases, I considered invented spelling acceptable as long as students were able to read what they wrote. Sometimes it is important to give students the much-needed opportunity to get as many of their ideas down on paper as possible, because the fear of being judged or not spelling perfectly can often stifle and discourage them from even attempting to write detailed stories in the first place. Try to work with them at whatever level they are at, then build from there. What you notice about their writing strengths and weaknesses may become teaching points for future lessons. You as the teacher can use your knowledge of grade-level standards as well as your overall assessment of students' abilities to determine what forms of writing are acceptable in your class.

English language learners or those students who have difficulty with spelling or finding appropriate vocabulary might be encouraged to start by drawing pictures to convey their stories, then add labels and simple sentences later. "Story paper," with small spaces for pictures followed by a few lines to write accompanying sentences is often good for this. You can create the drama books with this kind of paper in it, or staple the paper into the store-bought marble notebook pages. Some of my students drew colorful pictures labeled with one sentence or a few words. Others wrote whole paragraphs with no pictures at all. Both were acceptable forms of writing. This is part of what makes playmaking so enjoyable for the students: everyone can participate, regardless of how they communicate.

During the writing process, children would have periodic, individual conferences with me in which we discussed the content of their stories and I could help them add details. These conferences offer an opportunity to assess students' writing strengths and weaknesses and work more closely with them. The goal here is to help students enrich their stories by including many of the story elements you taught them about previously. Some things you may want to pay attention to are as follows:

- ◆ Does the student have one or two central characters (for example, the author or the author and his brother)?
- ◆ Did the student describe the setting or settings of the story?
- ◆ Is there a clear beginning, middle, and end?
- ◆ Does this drama book story relate to the theme the class has chosen?
- ◆ Is there enough dialogue, the words the people in the story actually said to one another?
- ◆ Does the story begin and end within a focused period of time (one afternoon or morning, as opposed to several days)?

Students also conferenced with each other. During these peer conferences, they would take turns sharing their stories, while the other person listened and then offered constructive criticism. This student-to-student interaction had been modeled in other content areas and practiced several times with my support, until students were able to conduct these sessions with relative independence.

Story Mapping

A story map can be described as a graphic organizer that shows the main elements of a story. The ones I have used most often with my students look like flowcharts that have boxes for "characters," "setting," and "plot" (or "beginning," "middle," and "end"). A sample story map follows.

STORY MAP
Characters (Who is the story mostly about?):
Setting (Where does the story happen? In what place?):
Problem/Conflict (What is bothering the main characters? What do they want?)
Solution/Resolution (How do the characters solve their problem? Do they get what they want?)
Beginning
Middle
End

As children became more adept at using this tool to understand the parts of a story, boxes for "problem/conflict" and "solution/resolution" were also included. These last two elements are important for children to comprehend when reading and writing stories or creating plays, because, often, these elements make a story interesting, move along the plot, and, depending on the problem, create dramatic tension. Children who can identify the problem/conflict and solutions/resolutions in stories often have a better overall understanding of what they have read.

We filled in story maps as a whole class to analyze and aid comprehension of stories that had just been read or told through exploration activities such as the read-aloud, storytelling, or drama book writing. Story mapping is also a great tool to use for discussions after trips to see plays or after classroom dramatizations. You can first model this for your students by showing them how you fill out a chart-sized story map using a story you have read to them many times. Then allow the children to help you fill out a story map for another story they may be familiar with or that was just read. Later in the playmaking process, you will help your students work with story maps in small groups in order to create and discuss stories to act out.

Field Trips

You can choose any trip that relates to your theme. For example, I took one class to see the exhibit "The Traditions of African Women" at the Schomburg Center for Research in Black Culture in Harlem. It showcased ceramics, clothing, and paintings, explaining how African women passed down the craft from one generation to the next for hundreds of years. The students made sketches of what they saw, brought the sketches back to class, and referred to them during our follow-up discussion about what we learned. This related to our family theme because it helped students deepen their understanding of how families work together cooperatively. The trip was also a great opportunity for parental involvement, as many parents accompanied us and assisted as chaperones.

Of course, trips to see plays geared toward children are particularly worthwhile. If the play is about your theme, it will help deepen the children's understanding in that area. Even if the play is not about your theme, your students will still become familiar with the elements of a play and performance. Before the play, prep your students by asking them to pay attention to how the performers bring characters to life. How do they use their faces? Their bodies? Their voices? How could you tell what the characters were feeling? How did the actors' performances make you feel? Since most plays are also stories, narratives brought to life, after the play you could also ask the same type of comprehension questions mentioned in the "Storytelling" and "Read-aloud" sections.

A trip to a play is also a chance to introduce and discuss roles and responsibilities involved in making a play. Playmaking vocabulary words such as "actor," "audience," "stage," "prop," "set," and "costume" will take on new meaning when students see all these things actually at work in front of them. Ask students later if they can identify how many actors were in a scene. What props were used to help the audience know that the scene was set outdoors (or in a kitchen, or a restaurant)? What did you notice about the costumes? How did the costumes help you understand more about the characters? How would you have changed the props or costumes to make the scene or play more realistic? What could the actors do to make the scene more realistic?

In addition to plays outside of school, students will benefit from attending plays other classes perform within school during assemblies or other special events. Seeing fellow students perform, especially those around their age, may boost their confidence and enthusiasm for doing so themselves. Recorded plays can also be borrowed from the local library or rented from a video store and viewed in the classroom.

Group Discussion

It bears repeating that discussion should be a part of all the activities mentioned in this book. It is an important part that aids your students' understanding of the theme and the playmaking process, whether discourse takes place between you and the student or when children talk with one another. Listening to your students can help you identify concepts they grasp well and others that may need reinforcement. Giving children the opportunity to express themselves verbally also supports oral language development, lets them know you value their opinion, and gives them a sense of ownership in the playmaking process. I observed that some of the richest student-to-student conversation occurred during peer conferences about drama book writings and when they shared story maps they had created as frameworks for dramatizations. The exchange of information during this time is part of what makes playmaking so student driven and empowering for young people.

Graphic Organizers

The story map mentioned above is just one of several graphic organizers you can use to deepen students' understanding of the theme of your play and the playmaking process. Visual aids will capture students' attention, can be used to record their responses during discussion, and can remain posted on large chart paper to help students remember what they learned about their theme. They can also be used as formal and informal assessment tools during and after many of these activities. Some examples of visual aids include simple lists; Venn diagrams to compare and contrast characters, settings, or thematic ideas; or the K-W-L strategy (Ogle, 1986) in which a three-column chart helps students think about and list what they *know*, *want* to know, and have *learned* about a theme.

3.2: CREATING STORIES

After your students have thoroughly explored their theme through a variety of activities, including sharing entries from their drama books, it is time to help them collaborate with one another to create short stories that reflect what they have learned and experienced.

By now, they are already familiar with the main elements of a story from the story mapping they did during their exploration activities. For this reason, I use story mapping again, this time as a graphic organizer to create stories in groups. Up to this point, story maps were used for breaking down a story that had just been read, but for the purposes of this phase of playmaking, it is used to build a story that we want to tell. Eventually, these stories will transform into the ones enacted for our play.

I first model this process with the whole class by posting a chart-sized story map I have prepared in advance, then I have the students dictate how they want to fill in the blanks for a story we make up as we go along. For example, the conversation might begin as follows:

TEACHER: Let's think of two main characters for our story. Who are they?

STUDENT #1: A brother and sister.

TEACHER: Okay. Let me write that down (teacher writes this in the "character" section of the story map). What are their names?

STUDENT #2: The brother's name is Timothy.

STUDENT #3: I think the sister's name should be Chantall.

TEACHER: Thank you. I will add this to our story map (teacher writes the names of these characters in the story map).

The teacher continues to guide this discussion in order to elicit suggestions for each part of the story (character, setting, problem, solution/resolution, beginning, middle, end, title), writing down the consensus of the class in the appropriate places, until the story map is complete. If at any time the class seems greatly divided about what should go on the story map, you could guide a brief discussion, allowing both sides of the issue to tell why they think a particular idea should be included on the map. Afterwards, you might take a vote that everyone agrees will be binding, and then move ahead. Most times, students are satisfied knowing that there will be other opportunities to create stories so that more ideas from other children can be included.

After this process is modeled, students are placed in small groups of four to six people, and each group is given a large story map on chart paper to use in creating their own story. Depending on the size of your class, you can end up with three to five groups that will each work simultaneously. It helps if you have already established roles and responsibilities for group work—such as recorder, materials person, and presenters—before you commence this activity. Some groups will be able to complete their maps right away, while others will take more time. Encourage students to refer to the stories in their drama books if they need ideas. Also urge groups to try and keep their stories to one setting, two at the most (as opposed to the story starting at home, then moving to school, then the library; or starting Wednesday afternoon, then continuing Thursday morning into Thursday evening). Circulating from group to group and observing the completion of the story maps will help you assess how well students understand the nature of story elements.

Once story maps are completed, the whole class gathers together to hear each group take a turn presenting the story maps they created. This is a great opportunity for developing oral language and critical thinking skills, since students are not speaking only in response to the teacher but are carrying on a focused discussion in response to one another. After each group presents, the rest of the class (the audience) gets to make comments and ask a few questions that explore the group's reasoning and even expand on ideas and plotlines in the story presented. The group that created the story has the opportunity to respond and, in the end, may decide whether to modify their story map based on this exchange.

Of course, filling in a story map is not the same as creating a fully fleshed-out story. However, in playmaking each completed story map may serve as a framework for improvisational activities in the next phase, "Acting Out."

3.3 ACTING OUT

After students have worked together collectively to create stories based on their experiences with and knowledge of the chosen theme, it is time to bring those stories to life through dramatization. This section of the guide touches on how you can help your students do this through theatre games, pantomime, and improvisation.

For the purposes of playmaking, I think of dramatization as yet another way for students to explore their theme and tell their stories. In some ways, the field trips, reading, and drama book writing are ways to lead up to and enrich the quality of the dramatizations. At the same time, by acting out theme-related stories, children will get a different perspective on the issues involved in the theme.

As you will see, the stories they share in the course of these activities, particularly the story mapping, provide the situations, structure, and motivation for the dramatizations ahead. Performances may take place in a clear area of your classroom that you have set up just for playmaking, or a space you have already established for your meeting area (refer to "Getting Started").

Warm-Up Activities/Theatre Games

As you can imagine, at first not every child is comfortable speaking in front of a group. You may have a student who is a real ham and jumps at the chance to perform, while others may be expressive in a small group but at a total loss for words in front of the whole class. In addition, since there is no formal script, some students may feel pressure to make up ideas and bring them to life on the spot.

These are some of the reasons I introduce my students to the world of dramatic performance by warming them up through theatre games. The purpose of engaging students in class-wide warm-up activities is to help them loosen up, relieve nervousness and tension, and become comfortable with the concept of showing stories and concepts with the body, voice, and mind.

Some educators may choose to do these activities before pantomime and improvisation of the stories that students have created. Others may use these activities as an intervention when they notice students' movements are somewhat stiff or uninspired. I most often began each playmaking session with these activities as a "do now," or warm-up, in order to build and reinforce performance skills throughout the process. Either way, you will notice improvement in the quality of your students' performance, and some students may become much less inhibited after participating in these activities. The following are a few warm-ups I have done with my students over the years, but if you would like more information on other theatre games and warm-ups, you may refer to the bibliography at the end of this book.

May-Mee-Mah-Mo-Moo

This activity helps students loosen up their facial muscles and exercise their voices. Have all of the students stand and repeat the following set of five syllables—may, mee, my, mo, moo—making sure to hold the last syllable "moo" as long as they can. Some clever students may notice that what they are saying encompasses many short and long vowel sounds. Bring their attention to how the mouth stretches and changes for each phrase, and encourage them to exaggerate this as they do it over and over, taking a deep breath before each sequence. Have them practice the phrase together as class, sometimes softly, other times loudly.

The Growing Trees

This is a wonderful activity for relaxing and stretching both the body and the imagination. Have everyone stand, either by their desks or in your playmaking area. Tell them, "We are going to grow into a whole forest right in the classroom! However, first we must become seeds in the ground by squatting down as low as we can, with our heads tucked in and our arms wrapped around us as tightly as possible." Once your students have done this, tell them to show you how they begin to "grow" into a tree by standing up slowly. Watch as the children give their own unique interpretation, uncurling themselves at different rates of speed, becoming taller and taller, until they are standing with their arms stretched out in various ways like branches. Have them stay in their position and peek over at one another to see what types of trees are near them. You can suggest that children who are still balled up near the ground grow by standing up, or tell some children to "Show your branches" or ask them, "Can you make your arms into branches?"

Once they have become "trees," you can have them repeat the activity or extend it by saying that the weather has suddenly changed. First you can tell them to show you their tree-selves in the wind, and notice how the students sway to and fro. Just remind them to keep their feet planted, because these are their roots. You can make the weather calm again, or bring in a thunderstorm or even a tornado.

Stage Direction "Simon Says"

This is a great game for getting students accustomed to moving around and using the whole stage, as well as reinforcing their memory of stage directions. It is similar to the game Simon Says, except that a small group of participants (four to six children) begin by standing center stage. The rest of the class observes as the audience. The teacher (or a student) calls out the name of a place on the stage, and the participants must go there. For example, if "stage right" is called out, all the participants should move to their right, still staying in the center row of the stage. Next, the teacher might call out "move down stage," in which case the participants should move forward and closer to the audience, while still staying on the right side of the stage. The different directions can be called out five more times or until the group misses a direction, and then another group can have a turn.

What Is It?

This game is like charades, except that each participant takes turns using a simple object in a different way. You may demonstrate this by using something from the prop box, such as a cardboard tube. Hold it up and say, "This looks like an old paper towel tube. But it's not really a paper towel tube...." Then throw up an imaginary ball and pretend to hit it with the tube. Ask "What is it?" The students should guess "a baseball bat." Pass the tube to one of the students and let each one take turns acting out new identities for the object, while the other participants try to figure it out. For example, that same tube could become a rolling pin, an astronomer's telescope, a large straw, a can of soda, or a canon.

Stage Traffic

This activity prepares children for coordinating their movements in a small space by becoming aware of the other actors who share the stage with them. Have the students stand in a circle and tell them they must walk across the room to a different place in the circle without bumping into one another. There will probably be some laughs and giggles at first, but with practice they will become more and more coordinated. You can vary this activity by asking students to walk while exhibiting an emotion like happiness, fear, anger, sadness, surprise, etc.

Pass Along

This game offers a fun way to explore both the actions and thinking that can be involved in pantomime. Have all the students sit down in a circle and tell them you will pass around an imaginary object. They will not be able to really see it, but they will be able to show what it is by the way they use it. The first few times you do this activity, you may want to tell the students what the object is. For example, you could say, "I'm going to pass along a basketball." First, touch the surface of the imaginary basketball in front of you to establish its shape and size for the students. Then, you could pretend to pick it up and bounce it before passing it to a student next to you. You might encourage the students to try and do something different from what the last person did with the object, but the main idea is to maintain the perception of the shape, size, and even weight of the object from person to person. In the case of the basketball, one child might bounce it, the next might roll it to the next student, another might balance it on his head, while another might try to slam dunk it into an imaginary hoop. As students become more comfortable with this activity, you may have a child create the object and start the pass, or you may decide not to name the object at first, but let students figure it out by the way each person interacts with it. After the object has been passed around to every student, you can discuss what was different about the way students used or interacted with the object. Ask them how they could tell what the object was. Which gestures or actions made the object seem the most real?

Pantomime

Simply put, pantomime (or mime) refers to the art of acting out a story without words, only body movements, gestures, and facial expressions. Performers such as Marcel Marceau of France and silent film star Charlie Chaplin were highly skilled at pantomime. Some dramatic arts educators see pantomime as simply a warm-up or skill-building activity. Indeed, practice with pantomime can help children become more comfortable with their bodies, and they may come to use pantomime to convey ideas central to the story they are acting out. Through pantomime, students can create a sense of space, environment, mood, and objects. In the process, students must consider spatial relationships, height, depth, distance, and even speed. However, it should be noted that pantomime is an art form in and of itself whose roots stretch back hundreds of years and took a variety of forms in different cultures and eras. In ancient Rome, for example, pantomime involved one performer acting all the parts and action while a chorus sang the story.

In the context of the playmaking process, pantomime can be part of warm-up activities (such as "Pass Along" and "Growing Trees"), but it is also a way for students to act out whole stories before they improvise these stories with spoken words. This is because it encourages students to *show* the details and emotions involved in a story, not just rely on speaking to *tell* the story, a skill we may want our students to master in their writing as well. Movements and gestures are usually bigger and more exaggerated than the way those same actions would be done in "real life" off the stage.

You can have students pantomime stories individuals wrote in their drama books or tales created by a small group that have been discussed through story mapping. To start, I usually acted as narrator, using the story map or a student's drama book writing as a guide to retell the story, while the children who were selected to act it out used my words as prompts to do appropriate movements. For example, if I were to say, "One morning, Keisha went to the bathroom to brush her teeth," the child playing Keisha would hold an imaginary toothbrush in her hand, moving her fist up and down in front of her teeth. I did not have to tell the student to make these particular movements; the actions were implied by the words in the narration.

I continued to narrate whole stories while the players pantomimed, and the rest of the class acted as "active audience" members. This meant that while some students were performing pantomime, the other students were asked to be particularly observant, not just watching for entertainment (although that will inevitably happen, as you will see when they laugh and make "oohs" and "aahs"), but paying close attention to the performers, what they did, and how they did it. After the pantomime performances were finished, I would ask the students questions such as:

- How did the actors show feelings?
- What did the actors do with their faces?
- What did the actors do with their hands?
- How did you know when the actors' feelings or mood changed?
- Was there another way that the actors could have used their face or body movements to show that feeling? Can you demonstrate this?
- How did the actors show the setting? How could you tell where they were?

Not only does this keep the students who are not performing interested in what is going on, but it also helps spur ideas about what to do (or what they choose not to do) when it is their time to perform. Additionally, the thinking that the active audience does is closely related to the language arts skill of making inferences when reading. Many times, ideas and concepts are not obvious in text, but instead implied through the main character's actions. Figuring out what feelings or ideas are implied during this pantomime activity is an experience teachers can refer back to as a way to encourage students to use that same skill when reading books independently.

Later, as my students got used to this format, they were able to act as narrators of their own stories while others acted them out. Of course, the difference in this case is that the narrator is often saying "I"—as in, "I went outside to play with my friends."

After each pantomime, we continued to have discussions about what we saw, particularly the ways the actors were able to tell the story without words, movements they used, how fast or slow they moved, etc. I also asked the children to suggest and demonstrate alternate gestures that might have conveyed the same ideas. As often as possible, different children were allowed to play the same roles and do whatever movements they felt appropriate.

For example, if a narrator said, "Jean-Paul sat at the table and ate his cereal," one student might act this out by pretending to pick up an imaginary spoon, dip it in an imaginary bowl, lift the spoonful of cereal to his open mouth, and then simulate chewing. When that same story is narrated again with a different student in the role of "Jean-Paul," he might simply pick up the imaginary bowl, put it to his mouth, toss his head back and pretend to take big gulps of cereal without using a spoon. Which version of that scene is correct? In a way, both. This is due to the very nature of the pantomime activities, which empower children to make their own choices based on their interpretation of the story and the characters in it. The first child may have based his pantomime on how he himself eats cereal in real life in his home. The second child may also be basing his performance on real life, if he can get away with doing that at his family breakfast table. It is also possible that based on other details in the story, the second child believed "Jean-Paul" to be very hungry at that moment, or rough and gluttonous in general, so he made a choice to use a eating style that reflected this. This is why after each pantomime enactment, teachers should not only question the active audience, but also ask the actors to discuss the reasoning behind the choices they made.

However, there are limits. For example, if a different student played "Jean-Paul" and pretended to use a knife and fork, this would be inappropriate because (usually) a bowl of cereal cannot be eaten that way; the milk and flakes would just slip through the spaces in the fork. Keep in mind that this point of correction may not be necessary for you to state, but can be left up to the active audience with your guidance, training, and careful questioning. After the scene is complete, you might ask them, "How did the actor show that he was eating a bowl of cereal?" This is a recall question, similar to when children are reading and asked to recall facts or details about a passage. This is not the time for children to offer opinions about whether the actor's interpretation was right or wrong. Next, after you have established what was done (an imaginary fork and knife were used), you could ask the following types of questions:

◆ Is that how you usually eat cereal?
◆ What would happen if you used a fork and knife to eat cereal in real life?
◆ What could the actor have done to make that scene even more believable?
◆ Could you demonstrate how you would do that scene?

The point is that you want to get the students thinking about the performance without imposing your own opinions on them or putting anybody down. Of course, some children can be very sensitive and uncomfortable when others talk about their actions no matter what you do, but again, careful lines of questioning can make all the difference. Try to talk about the actions and not so much about the actor. Start by asking the active audience what actions or ideas they thought were conveyed well. If they cannot come up with a compliment, then you can offer one. You might decide, instead, to ask the actors these types of questions so they are empowered to think about and modify their own actions—not because someone else told them to do so, but because they figured it out themselves. Once children are used to thinking about and analyzing performances in this way, you may want to guide the actors and active audience members to start speaking directly to one another, reducing your involvement little by little. Some audience members may have questions about what they saw, so you might teach them how to phrase their questions. For example, you could encourage your students to use comments like the following:

◆ I really believed you when you did.....because......
◆ When you did......it reminded me of......
◆ Why did you decide to do......?

- May I make a suggestion?
- Can you think of another way you could have done that?
- How did you come up with that idea?
- I didn't understand when you did..... Could you please explain that?
- It was hard for me to believe that because...........

It may take time, but the more you model asking these types of questions yourself, and maybe even posting these verbal prompts on chart paper in your classroom, the more students will move toward constructive criticism.

A word about props: You will probably notice students pretending to use certain imaginary items that are implied by the narration of the story being pantomimed (such as the spoon in the aforementioned cereal pantomime). This shows a great deal of imagination on your students' part. Allowing them to do this will help them develop their abstract thinking and motor skills in a creative way. However, you may feel the urge to aid them by allowing them to use real objects in their pantomime, or your students themselves might make this request. If so, feel free to introduce the prop box at this time. Remember, your prop box is filled with ordinary items students can use to help them perform. For more on how the prop box can be used, see "Set Design, Props, and Costuming."

Improvisation and Adding Dialogue

Eventually, I suggested that students start using some words, phrases, or even simple sounds to help convey ideas in the stories they performed. For example, if the story called for Malik to eat a delicious meal at the dinner table, I might suggest that as he pantomimes eating with a fork, he does something else to convey this idea. I might say, "Malik, is there anything we could hear that would let us know you think this food is delicious?" Malik might then decide to say, "Mmm ..." during his pantomime. As you give other actors the chance to play the same role, you will notice different interpretations. Rafael might actually add a phrase, such as "Mmm ... this spaghetti is really good!" The more that children play out the stories and observe others, the more comfortable and creative they will get with movement, and eventually they will add appropriate words. Once words become a regular part of their enactment, by definition, it ceases to be a pantomime. This is one way to transition your students into improvisations of stories.

Improvisation (or improv) occurs when actors portray characters in a given situation spontaneously, with minimal or no planning. In the "Create Stories" phase, students worked in groups to create the outline of a story using a story map. Now each story mapping group of four to six students can confer with one another in a corner of the room to think of ways to act out those stories or new story mapped tales through improvisation. As stated earlier, the story map they created provides the situation and structure (setting and plot) for your students to work within, while the dialogue and characterization come about naturally from the students based on what they feel will move the story along. The role of narrator is one of many that the students in the group can now take on themselves or leave out.

The first time students confer with one another in this way, you will need to circulate from group to group and offer varying degrees of guidance and support. During this time, ensure that each group tries to complete the following five tasks:

1) Refer to the story map and decide on the main elements of the story.

2) Assign roles and responsibilities such as narrator or prop/set designer, and decide who will play specific characters. Students may need to take on more than one of these roles, depending on the number of children in the group.

3) Decide how they will represent the setting in the given space and where they want to place props.

4) If time permits, do a quick practice or run-through of what they will actually do when they perform. The performance of the improv should take anywhere from five to eight minutes.

5) They should consider "blocking," meaning determining where on the stage actors will stand in relation to each other, when they should move, who will walk on stage first, etc. You may not want to encourage your students to do this if you feel it diminishes the spontaneity of the activity. However, practicing the first few times they engage in improvisation may help build confidence in children who are unsure of themselves.

Do not expect this planning or the initial performance to be perfect. It is not supposed to be. The quality of the improvisations will improve through planning and performing them over and over.

After groups are given brief time to plan, the whole class gathers together to watch each group perform. When it is a group's turn, they set up the "stage" for their scene by placing props and set dressing, such as chairs, pillows, books, or boxes where they need to be when the scene begins. Actors and narrators then take their places on or off stage and hold this position until the narrator or another designated student calls out "scene" or "action" to signal the beginning of the scene.

Just as they did during the pantomime activities, actors in the group may be prompted to move about the stage and progress through the story by the narrator's words—only this time, the narrator does not tell what is said; the actors create the character's words themselves. When two characters talk in response to each other, it is called "dialogue." When groups perform, students make up appropriate dialogue based on what makes sense in the situation the narrator is presenting. For example:

NARRATOR: Lisa's mother wanted her to wear a green sweater, but Lisa didn't want to.
MOTHER: Here, Lisa, try on this sweater.
LISA: No, I don't want to!
MOTHER: Why not?
LISA: I hate green.

The dialogue above is from an actual improvisation performed by a group of seven- and eight-year-olds. The children made up all of the words. Nobody told the child playing the mother to question why Lisa didn't want to wear the sweater; in that child's mind, it just seemed to be the logical thing to do. Another child in the mother role might have decided to be more authoritative and say,

MOTHER: It doesn't matter what you want. You have to wear it because I said so.

Again, much of the dialogue depends on the plot that the group mapped out, as well as how the group and the actors perceive the characters' personality traits. Either response from the mother character may be acceptable as long as it makes sense in the situation and helps move the story along.

When the story is complete and the actors are done performing, the narrator can simply say "The end," and everyone in the group (whether they performed or not) takes a bow. They will stay in the stage area as the active audience shares their questions and comments, similar to the way students spoke with one another after pantomimed performances. You may use a story map to guide conversations, particularly if you want your students to pay attention to story elements. See if they can identify the characters and their relationship to each other. Can they describe the setting? How would they describe the problem or conflict, as well as its resolution? You may refer to the questions you asked students after field trips to plays, such as those dealing with how actors used props and set dressing to convey their characters and the setting. During this interaction, students can work together to think critically about the story, review how it was brought to life, and brainstorm ways to make it better.

It is important to note that making an improvisation "better" is based on the idea that a good improvisation is one in which the actors make choices about words and actions that are realistic and logical for the characters they portray. Therefore, your role as an educator is to help students think about not only how they would act in real life, but how the character they are portraying would act (and react) in the situation being played out in the improvisation. Some of this will be brought to light by the questions and comments from the active audience. However, if it is not, one way for you to facilitate this discussion is to explore each character's traits.

You may have already discussed character traits with your students as a way of describing key aspects of a character's personality or tendencies. The following chart contains examples of some of the many character traits you and your students may have noticed when watching plays or in books during read alouds, guided reading, or shared reading time. Note that character traits are related to, but different than, feelings (such as happy, sad, scared, annoyed, etc).

SOME CHARACTER TRAITS		
adventurous	arrogant	bossy
brave	clumsy	considerate
courageous	cowardly	curious
dishonest	friendly	funny
generous	gentle	grouchy
hard-working	honest	impatient

kind	lazy	mean
messy	mischievous	neat
obedient	patient	rude
selfish	shy	thrifty

I have always found it helpful to have a character trait chart posted in the classroom to remind children of the words we can use to describe a character and what they mean. Sometimes I would place a column in the chart that referenced a particular character from a book we had read that exemplified that trait.

WE CAN CALL A CHARACTER....	...IF THEY DO THIS	JUST LIKE....
Brave	Do something even though it could be dangerous or they are afraid	Katy Sue in *The Recess Queen* by Alexis O'Neil

Here is an even simpler version of the headings:

TRAIT	ACTIONS	CHARACTER

Considering character traits can be beneficial for many reasons. In playmaking, understanding or deciding on a character's primary traits will help inform a student's choices about how he will portray that character. Furthermore, identifying character traits is important in language arts development. When reading, it offers insights into characters' "motivation," the reasons why the characters do the things they do in the story. Knowing a character's traits can also help readers make predictions about what a character is likely to do in the next part of a story. It aids the craft of writing because it helps children focus on creating appropriate scenarios and plots for the main characters they are writing about.

While the ability to identify character traits is an important skill that can be developed, I have found that it can be challenging for young readers to master for three main reasons:

1) Children may not be encouraged to constantly pay special attention to what a character does, says, thinks or feels as they read.

2) Children are not explicitly taught to use what they notice about the character's actions as evidence of that character's traits.

3) Although children may have a sense of a character's personality and tendencies, they may lack the vocabulary to adequately describe them.

Certainly, some of your students will demonstrate a natural aptitude for this type of inferential thinking. However, before we can expect them to utilize this skill independently and with some level of automaticity, the three aforementioned issues must be addressed.

The playmaking process offers children a unique opportunity to practice the thinking required to master this skill. As they create, perform, watch, and discuss improvisations, students actually experience and analyze characters' actions in a multisensory way that facilitates understanding differently than reading text off a page alone.

One way to discuss character traits after an improvisation is to first talk about what students perceive a character's traits are or should be, then use that information to enhance the actor's performance. For example, after a performance you could ask the active audience, "What words would you use to describe this character?" After a few audience members have responded, you may then ask, "What did the actor say or do to make you think that?" If, for example, students say that she is "shy," then the question becomes, "How can you tell that the character is shy? What did the actor do or say that made you think that?" You may also ask the actor what trait she feels best describes the character she portrayed. From here, some additional things for your class to consider are as follows:

- ♦ Was the trait the actor intended to convey the same as what the audience perceived (For example, did the audience feel the character was sneaky, while the actor meant the character to come off as adventurous)? If so, what were some things the actor did to make that clear? If not, what could the actor have done to make his intent clearer?
- ♦ Was the way the character was portrayed appropriate for the story and situation (For instance, in an improvisation where the main character is supposed to be distraught over losing a teddy bear, did the character seem too cheerful or aloof?)

Of course, just as in real life, most people exhibit more than one trait at the same time depending on the situation, so it is great if your students notice this.

Another approach is to work in the reverse. First, review the character's actions in the story and then use that in a discussion to draw a conclusion about what character trait is implied by those actions. You could ask the active audience, "What are some things this character did and said?" Then ask, "What does that make you think about this character?" Or more specifically, "What word would you use to describe a person that does that?"

Whichever way you approach the discussion, the group who put that improvisation together can use this feedback to then decide whether to modify their improvisation to reflect the characters' true natures and the main idea of their skit.

These considerations closely mirror the skill of revision in the writing process. When students are stuck with their writing, educators can refer back to their playmaking experience and remind them that just as they reconsidered the actor's actions to fit the character and the situation, they can also revise their writing so the characters say and do things that reveal the traits and ideas the student writers intend.

Some educators may want to record the improvisational performances and then review the footage with the class in order to facilitate this post-discussion. The advantage is that video can be paused or cued to points of interest. It offers a way to reflect on the action and dialogue immediately after the performance, at another time of the school day, or even later in the week if necessary (although I would highly recommend having post-discussions as soon after performances as possible, so that students' ideas and opinions are fresh in their minds). If you are interested in recording but are unsure how it works or do not have the equipment, this may be a great opportunity for parental involvement. You may find that one or more students' parents are willing to lend video equipment, teach you how to use it, or even volunteer to do the taping themselves at a pre-arranged time. Of course, every school and district has its own policies about recording and informed consent, so make sure that you check with school administration and obtain permission from parents before doing recording of any kind.

3.4 SET DESIGN, PROPS, AND COSTUMES

Props (an abbreviation of "properties") are any items that actors handle and use on stage. Costumes are the clothes actors wear on stage and can often give the audience clues about a character's personality, age, and lifestyle. Sometimes a prop, such as a scarf or a wristwatch, can also be considered part of a costume. Items used to decorate and give an idea of the setting, such as a desk, couch, or plant are considered scenery or set dressing.

The spontaneity inherent in improvisational performance means that props and costumes are not always necessary. Many times, children's own creativity, words, or pantomimes are sufficient to convey the story. However, props can save the day when a child is in a rut. As theatre historian and educator Dr. Nellie McCaslin (1997) states, "if children experience difficulty in getting into character, a piece of a costume may sometimes be all that is needed to provide the necessary incentive" (p. 74).

If and when your students choose to make use of props, costuming, and set dressing, then their earlier trips to see plays and other performances during the exploration phase will become very useful now. They can recall the types of objects that were part of the set and that the actors used to bring the story to life. Important aspects of the set will also be suggested by reviewing the details of the story itself. Students can refer to the "setting" section of the story map to remind them where the improvisation takes place and to get ideas about what the set should look like. Below are some questions you may want to pose to your students to get them thinking about appropriate props and scenery:

- Is the story set indoors or outdoors?
- In daytime or nighttime?
- In a house or an apartment building?
- And is it big or small?
- Is the story set in the city or the country?
- What season is it?

One of my first-grade classes actually enacted three different stories about family, so there were three different sets. One story was set in a living room. Everyone in the class agreed that most living rooms have something to sit on. However, there was a question as to whether that thing would be a couch or a recliner. In this instance, I facilitated a discussion on the topic to help us choose the appropriate object. Eventually the children decided on a sofa, because it would accommodate the two main characters if they wanted to sit on it at the same time. Another story was set in a bedroom in the morning time. This suggested that we would need a bed, which we made by putting three chairs together. A parent brought in chair cushions to make this prop more comfortable.

As for costumes, the time of this same story (the morning) also suggested that the characters should wear pajamas, but for the purposes of improvisation, this was not necessary. For most of the rehearsals, everyone wore regular school clothes or got creative with a few items from the prop box, and they were still able to get into character. Once your class has decided on a specific improvisation to perform for their show, any costumes should be put aside and made available for rehearsals and the day of the performance. Parents can be encouraged to contribute what they can. For example, parents of the children doing the bedroom improvisation sent them to school with their pajamas, slippers, and even a pillow. If they did not have pajamas from home that they felt comfortable using, we could have gotten some from a thrift shop. Otherwise, children's actions (yawning, making the bed, etc.) would have been enough to indicate that it was morning in a bedroom and that they had been asleep.

Besides items already in the classroom or brought from home, students were also allowed to choose items from the prop box, a container of common objects set aside and recycled specifically for playmaking. As mentioned in the "Getting Ready" section, this box can be made available throughout the playmaking process and offers a unique way to practice conservation. During one improvisation, some children used an empty cardboard box from the prop box to represent a television in the living room. Two small tissue-paper tubes were taped together and used as binoculars for a skit set in a park. A very creative group used my chalkboard erasers wrapped in foil from the prop box to represent the controllers used to play a video game.

Keep in mind that although a prop box is useful, your students do not have to rely on it. Sometimes my students opted instead to pantomime the objects that were in the setting. This sometimes makes children more comfortable, because they do not have to worry about cumbersome objects. Using their creativity and judgment, children can create whatever they need. As noted educator Gertrude Kerman (1961) points out, "the main thing to remember here is that too many props will confuse your player, while a few props will stimulate him" (p. 15). If a group of students actually assemble or create a prop that your class seems to use over and over, you may keep it assembled for future use in other improvisations or pantomimes. The chart on the next page offers a few suggestions on how some prop box items can be transformed.

Also remember that if some children show more of an affinity for set design than playacting, it is okay to allow them to take on this role. Just make sure they are allowed to take a turn on stage acting out a character so they can see for themselves what they are more comfortable with.

If you are artistically inclined or can collaborate with an art teacher, you may want to help your students create a backdrop for their performance. A backdrop can be a mural drawn or painted on a sheet of butcher paper or fabric that is large enough to cover the back or side wall where the children will perform. Its purpose is to convey a sense of the setting. The illusion of a neighborhood park can be created by drawing trees, grass, rocks, and swings as a backdrop. Backdrops and other types of scenery can also be created from large sheets of cardboard or foamboard used as either a backdrop or cut into the shape of something (such as a mailbox, car, or building), decorated, and propped up.

ITEMS	SCENERY, PROPS, OR COSTUMING
fabric	scarf, skirt, dress
sheets	window curtain, tablecloth, bedspread, sofa cover
cardboard box	television, table, plant pot, bookshelf, doghouse, gift
milk crates	large appliance (refrigerator, television), table, bookshelf, bench
paper or plastic plates	plate (of course), hat, shield, steering wheel, portrait
rope	dog leash, belt, lasso, fence
paper-towel or tissue-paper tubes	telescope, binoculars, lamp, flashlight, microphone

Note that having more than one setting means a change will have to take place at some point in the improvisation. This does not have to involve the daunting task of moving all props and scenery off the stage area and then dragging on the new items. My students realized that props used in one enactment could stay on stage and be reused or transformed for the next enactment. They also learned how to work together and took responsibility for making the transitions from scene to scene run smoothly. The children who acted in the first improvisation always rearranged the props and set them up for the children in the next improvisation. In this way, everyone took responsibility for being a sort of stagehand or prop master.

3.5 SCRIPTING

After practice with pantomime and replaying some of the same group improvisations several times, you and your students can now decide which group-created stories will be performed on the day of your show. Each story selected will become an act in the script you create with your class.

A basic script is a written record of what each character says in the order of the plot. It can also indicate some of the actors' movements or stage directions and other information, such as a description of the various settings and the titles of the different acts. After the script is completed, a copy can be made for each student in the class, but not necessarily for the purpose of word-for-word memorization. In the context of playmaking, the script acts simply as a guideline during rehearsals, reminding young actors of key points they must touch on to move the story along.

Creating the script is similar to shared writing, in that the students create the words and the teacher writes them down. However, rather than just taking dictation, during this session you will ask your students to review the improvisations and make decisions about what dialogue to keep and what to leave out, based on what makes the most sense, is most realistic, and advances the plot. You are also likely to find that your students will choose dialogue that is the most entertaining and interesting to perform. Some classes will think the dialogue is just fine, in which case you can write all the words down as-is. If you are comparing two versions of the same improvisation and a particular character says almost the same words in each one (even if it's a different actor portraying that character), that is a strong indication your students are comfortable with that wording, and a very good reason to keep it in the script. As the teacher, you are also part of the class, so feel free to make your own suggestions, but try to avoid dominating these sessions. You want your students to end up with dialogue they feel comfortable with and can say smoothly, because it contains culturally and developmentally appropriate vocabulary.

There are a number of ways for you to review the skits and conduct this type of discussion about the script. One way is to use a digital video camera to record enactments of each improvisation. After the recordings, review the tape with the whole class, while allowing your students to tell you which pieces of dialogue make the most sense and convey the ideas of the story best. You can pause the tape at the points that your students indicate, then write down the key words and phrases from that section before moving on. Alternately, you could also use a log sheet to record the exact place (hour, minute, second) in the tape that has dialogue students want to keep or remove.

Time (hour:minute:second)	Description	Notes
00 : 14 : 10	The Stroller Story	
00 : 25 : 57	The Game Trouble	
__ : __ : __		

This makes the dialogue easy to find if you decide to go over the tape again and transcribe it later. Do not feel daunted if you cannot capture and write down everything verbatim. The point is to jot down the key words and phrases that reflect the main ideas the actors want to get across.

If using video technology is not feasible, you may transcribe the words for the script by allowing each group to perform their skit and have them pause or "freeze" after a few words are said so you can quickly write them down. If most of the students agree that these words should be in the show, then allow the actors to "unfreeze" and continue for a few more lines before pausing again to write down more words. This may seem like a tedious process, but children often find the "freezing" part fun, particularly if you give the active audience the power to call out and freeze the action. They also like to take on the role of detectives, seeing who is the best at focusing their attention and listening very carefully to recall the specific words the actors just used. They have enjoyed seeing and hearing these enactments so many times that you may be surprised to find the audience knows the dialogue by heart!

Another option is to have each playmaking group present the dialogue from their improvisation while sitting together with the class. Remember, they have had fun enacting their stories so many times that the actors may easily recall what they said or want to say, and they can share this with the class. During the discussion, you can jot down the agreed-upon words on a notepad or big chart paper for all to see and type them later.

Whichever approach you use, remember to also ask students to confirm the essential stage directions, as well. Keep in mind that you are simply recording the directions and items already suggested by what the students created themselves during the course of their enactments.

Once you have collaborated with your students to transcribe the dialogue and some stage directions, you can now type this into the form of a script. Most scripts follow the same basic format. You will indicate which character is speaking by starting each line with that character's name in bold and/or capital letters, followed by a colon. The words a character speaks go after the colon. Therefore, if your students are acting out a story involving a teacher (Ms. Blake) and student (Lashay), their dialogue could appear in a script like this:

LASHAY: I brought you an apple today, Ms. Blake.

MS. BLAKE: Thank you! I will eat if for lunch.

In addition, you may also want to use parentheses to indicate simple stage directions, which props should be used at these moments, or key emotions the character must convey for the story to make sense.

> **LASHAY**: (She walks to Ms. Blake's desk smiling, with an apple in her hand.) I brought you an apple today, Ms. Blake.
>
> **MS. BLAKE**: (Takes the apple and puts it in her purse.) Thank you! I will eat if for lunch.

You may also indicate the setting of a particular scene with a simple line just before the dialogue.

> Setting: *Ms. Blake's second grade classroom, Monday morning*
>
> **LASHAY**: (She walks to Ms. Blake's desk smiling, with an apple in her hand.) I brought you an apple today, Ms. Blake.
>
> **MS. BLAKE**: (Takes the apple and puts it in her purse.) Thank you! I will eat if for lunch.

The play your class finally decides to script and perform may be based on a story created by only one group, or it could include the stories created by each group. If you choose to perform more than one group's story, then you can divide the script into acts. For example, in one class I worked with, a group performed a story they called "The Stroller Story," and another group performed a story called "The Game Trouble," all within the same show. It was noted in the script as.

> **Act 1: The Stroller Story.**

All the dialogue for "The Stroller Story" was written after this line. Then the story that was to be performed next was written in the script as

> **Act 2: The Game Trouble.**

The script for this particular class included four stories, which took less than forty-five minutes to perform all together. As stated previously, you have to decide with your class how many of your group-created stories will be performed the day of your show, but I would suggest trying to do every group's story, if possible. If that seems a bit much, see if you can script and rehearse a play with half the stories in the class (two or three) and perform that, and then script the other half separately and perform those on another date. Each story, or act, that is scripted should take no more than about 10 to 20 minutes to perform. Anything longer might indicate a need to work with your students on making the plot a bit more concise.

Although the characters featured in the script are based on ones your students have created and agreed upon, you may occasionally see the need to provide opportunities for other students to perform in the show. You can do this by creating more characters in a variety of ways. One method I used, in order not to totally change the plot, was to add more narrators, so instead of one or two students telling the story, maybe three or four students would stand together and speak the same lines. This way, you do not have to alter the plot or add character names to the script. Another approach is to incorporate spectators, friends, or relatives of the main characters. The nature of the scene will determine which type of character to add, as well as whether the character needs to speak. For example, consider the sample script in the

Appendix of this guide. As written, there are four characters: Narrator, Amanda, Katey (Amanda's little sister), and Mother. Two more students could participate as narrators. Amanda could have an additional younger sibling who also comes in. In that case, Katey's lines could now be divided between two actors instead of one. Finally, if both Mother and Father come into the room, then that adds yet one more character. In the end, you go from performance opportunities for four students to eight.

After the script is completed, distribute one copy to each student and review it with the class. This is a great way to familiarize them with what make plays a unique literary genre. Explore the structure of the play and ask students to notice the ways it differs from how text usually appears in a regular fiction book. If it is not mentioned, point out that the words each character says are shown on separate lines following the character's name and a colon. Ask them to describe how this is different than the way most books show that a character is speaking.

3.6 CASTING

By observing your students during improvisations, you will begin to notice that different students have different strengths, needs, and interests. This should be the main criterion by which students are cast and assume roles in the play. Most often, casting for the actual show is based on the same roles students assumed while engaged in group improvisations.

Note that not all roles in the play involve performance. In the process of doing improvisations with your students, you will identify a number of important roles besides acting, such as narrator, set designer, stagehand, or prop master. Unless your students have created enough characters for everyone in the class, establishing a variety of roles and responsibilities on and off the stage provides more opportunities for everyone to participate.

For example, you might observe that, after several opportunities with improvisation, Marisol is still not comfortable speaking in front of an audience. However, she may be very expressive with her body language. In this case, you may offer her an acting role with no lines to speak but plenty of physicality, such as a dancer, athlete, or bystander. You know that Ibrahim is wheelchair bound but has a very strong speaking voice. He could play the role of a demanding father speaking to his children from the living room couch. Better yet, rather than disregard the fact of his mobility, he could play the role of a demanding father who just happens to be in a wheelchair. One child in my class was very soft-spoken and had a speech impediment. Although she struggled to speak alone, when she spoke or sang songs with other children, she was much more comfortable and clear. Realizing this, I cast her along with three other children as narrators who said their lines in unison.

Also, resist the temptation to give English language learners (ELLs) only non-speaking roles. This is an opportunity to help them become comfortable speaking aloud, add to their contextual vocabulary, and practice fluency. If you are proficient in the home language of the child, you may even allow him or her to incorporate some phrases from this language into the dialogue where appropriate. This makes the scene reflect a multicultural community. Encourage them to use the exaggerated facial expressions, movement and gesture skills they learned during pantomime to help convey ideas while performing. Another idea is to partner ELLs with bilingual students proficient enough in English to help translate their ideas to you, the rest of the class, or even as a bilingual narrator of the scene. The point is to allow children to participate in areas of the production where they can use and build on their strengths and interests, as well as develop new skills in a way that fosters confidence.

As stated previously, children who show more interest in props and set design, should have the opportunity to take on these roles. These are not simply roles made up to accommodate children a teacher feels "just can't act," children who are shy about performing, or students who are "left over" after all the acting roles are taken. Some students may genuinely enjoy building, creating, moving, and manipulating props for scenes much more than acting in them. Furthermore, practice in creating sets, props, and costumes engages more kinesthetic learners, allows children to problem solve ("How can we best utilize this space and our prop box resources to convey the setting?"), and helps them develop a keener awareness of spatial relationships. If a student seems to have developed a great deal of skill in this area, use your judgment to ascertain whether this comes from true interest or some feeling of discomfort about being on stage. If it is the latter, you may want to encourage that student to keep trying to perform with one of the improvisational groups, or take on a role that does not require as much time on stage. These efforts should only go so far. You want to be sure that whatever role the student takes on, it is one he or she really wants to do, not solely your opinion of what the child should be doing.

3.7 REHEARSAL

In the context of playmaking, students rehearse by continuing to replay their improvised stories over and over, with the script acting as a guideline. In a way, students start rehearsing as soon as they begin to engage in improvisation. The difference between then and now is that by going through the "Scripting" phase, students have made a commitment to try and stick with certain key plot lines and dialogue, with minimal variation.

Eventually, students will become confident enough and sufficiently organized so that the story or theme of the play is conveyed much more clearly. It is at this point that the students are ready to present their improvisations in front of an audience. Students and teachers alike will witness this progression. You will notice that awkward stops and starts become less frequent. The quality of the dialogue becomes richer as children have time to think about the situations they are enacting. Their language and voices will become more expressive, going from staccato delivery of a line like, "I-am-happy-to-see-you" to "Wow! It's great to see you!" Your observations during this time will allow you to assess students' understanding of the playmaking process, expressive and receptive oral language skills, the issues involved with the theme, and other learning objectives.

In traditional theatre productions, this is the point where the script would be given to the actors to take home and memorize, then used during rehearsal in case they forgot a line of dialogue. In playmaking, however, the script serves primarily as a way for the students and teacher to keep track of the general ideas and dialogue the children decided on. Parents can use the script to guide their children at home in the same fashion. At no point during rehearsal are students expected to read directly from the script. Some children may want to refer to it to remember what they wanted to say, but most do not need it because the replaying of the improvisations has helped them internalize most of the dialogue and key concepts. Furthermore, the dialogue written in the script does not have to be strictly adhered to. For example, if the script reads

> **KEVIN**: Hey Tina, that game looks like fun. Can I play?
>
> **TINA**: No!

it is okay if the actors end up saying,

> **KEVIN**: Hey Tina, can I play?
> **TINA**: Uh … I don't think so.

The point is that the main idea came across: Kevin wanted to play the game, but Tina would not let him. It was most important that the students remembered the overall concept. As long as Tina remembers this, and Kevin in some way asks to play, she can give an appropriate reply.

On the other hand, if for some reason the children lost sight of this, the teacher could refer to the script and remind them of the overall concept. For example, what if Kevin said the following?

> **KEVIN**: Hey, Tina, that game looks fun.

Leaving out "Can I play?" or any other words that ask if he can join in means that Tina does not have a question to answer in order to establish a conflict and move the story along. However, this type of issue could be addressed in one of two ways:

♦ The teacher could refer to the script and remind Kevin of his line by saying, "What question do you want to ask?" or "What do you want her to do?" OR

♦ Without prompting, Tina might recognize Kevin's intent, even though he was not explicit, and adjust her dialogue accordingly, using a reply such as

TINA: Yeah, but you can't play!

In the first case, the teacher uses the script to "side-coach" the student. In the second case, a peer uses her knowledge of the overall idea to move the play along. The child playing Kevin was not compelled to read directly from the script in either case. Note that the teacher does not simply tell the student the "right" thing to say from the script. This is because when a teacher has confidence in the students' knowledge, the teacher will use questions that allow them to solve problems on their own.

If students will perform their show somewhere other than where you have been rehearsing, try to get some rehearsal time in the actual performance space before the day of the show so your students can become comfortable performing there. Depending on how much side-coaching you feel is necessary, you may not get to rehearse every skit in each rehearsal session. This is fine, because you can rehearse the other skits in the next session. However, as you draw closer to the performance date, you should start doing run-throughs and at least one dress rehearsal. A run-through involves performing all the skits in sequence from the beginning to the end of the play without actors stopping and without any side-coaching from you. A dress rehearsal is similar, except that all costuming and props are used. These types of rehearsals help students feel what it will be like on the day of the show. They also allow students to develop smooth transitions by establishing where to go or stand offstage and what to do with themselves and their props once a scene or act is over and another one begins. They will also learn how to be quiet and listen for cues. Once run-throughs and dress rehearsals start to take place, everyone has to be in their places, just as on the day of the show; no one is merely a spectator.

As mentioned previously, your classroom can act as the performance space. Many times, my students actually moved the desks in the classroom for rehearsals and the day of the performance, creating an area in the back of the room with chairs for the audience and a clear area in front for the stage.

If you still choose to use a big auditorium (more than 75 seats), it will be difficult to do the show without microphones. Children's voices, even those that seem loud in a small classroom, can sound weak when sound dissipates in such a large space. Actors should not have to actually hold microphones on stage, but instead, microphones should be placed in strategic spots where they can pick up the voices of all the actors. Enlist the assistance of any school staff that handles staged events or technical equipment. If using a microphone becomes too awkward or voices still cannot be heard, consider performing in a different space.

Whether you use a large auditorium, smaller space, or classroom, you still want to go through some vocal projection exercises with your students. This is important because sometimes children are under the mistaken impression that if the person next to them on stage can hear them, then everyone else in the room can hear them, too. Also remind students that just as they exaggerate movements in pantomime to make the effect and ideas clearer, they may have to exaggerate the volume of their voices on stage. They must speak abnormally louder than they would in "real life," but without seeming to yell. Some teachers may model this by using their "teacher voice" as an example.

Although the pacing for playmaking is flexible, it is important for the teacher to use knowledge of the class and his or her students' capacities to gain a general idea of when they will be ready to perform. Setting a performance date can act as a motivator for students during rehearsal, helping them to set personal goals for themselves no matter what role they are playing. Generally, I find that the rehearsal period takes about five to seven 45-minute sessions, from the time the script is decided on to the actual performance in front of an audience.

3.8 PERFORMANCE

You have guided your students on an amazing journey through the playmaking process, helping them learn more about themselves and their chosen theme while developing skills they can use in other areas of their school and social lives. You have been observing your students through this process and making formal and informal assessments throughout, and hopefully you have learned new and surprising things about your students and their abilities.

Now it is time for your students' final performance, the culminating activity for this playmaking project. You should explain to your students that this is a time to share all the great things they have learned with an audience other than themselves. You may want to let them know that, in a way, they are also like teachers, educating the audience about important issues around the theme they have explored. Most important of all, you will want to tell them how proud you are of them because of how they have worked together and all they have accomplished.

Prior to the performance, you will need to do a few things to prepare. Have any props or special costuming prepared and stored in a designated cubby, closet, box, shelf, or backstage area prior to the performance and accessible on the day of the show. Engage your students in some fun warm-up activities several minutes before showtime to help them relax. Some vocal warm-ups can also be helpful. Remind students that nothing is ever perfect and if they stumble, stutter, or feel they have made a mistake, just keep going as best they can. On the day of the show, I also like to bring my students to the performance space early enough that we can do one last uninterrupted run-through of the play.

Give parents the opportunity to be involved. They can help with run-through rehearsals in order to be better prepared to assist on the day of the show. Backstage, they can calm students' nerves and help them switch costumes and sets.

If you like, you can make a simple, one-page program with the title of the play, the names of the students involved, and perhaps a few words from you or the students about the play or what everyone gained from participating in the playmaking process. You may designate students to act as ushers on the day of the show and be responsible for greeting audience members as they arrive, giving them programs and showing them to their seats.

The time of the performance should be as convenient for attendees as possible. Some teachers may want to have two performances of the play, one in the morning and one in the afternoon, to accommodate the schedules of invited parents and other family members. You will also want to share this performance with the rest of the school community. For one of my first-graders' playmaking performances, a pre-kindergarten class was invited in the morning and a second-grade class in the afternoon. We even videotaped the performance as a way to record and review our work, and to possibly share with the other classes that could not attend. If you choose to do this, check your school's policy on video recording and make sure you obtain signed permission slips from parents.

PART 4:
FOLLOW-UP AND ASSESSMENT

We often think of assessment as involving quizzes, multiple-choice tests, and the conferring of letter or number grades. However, the experiential, project-based nature of playmaking offers you many other unique opportunities to gather and interpret information in order to learn more about your students. This can be accomplished through your observations, discussions, and interactions with them throughout the entire process, not just at the final performance. You can then use that information to better understand how your students learn, monitor their growth and achievement in a variety of areas, check their understanding of the theme, inform your instruction, and make meaningful connections to other subject areas, particularly English language arts.

For example, after an improvisation or final performance, you can facilitate a discussion with students about what went well and what did not. Ask them what it felt like to perform in front of an audience. You could also ask what they learned about the theme that they did not know before, or how it might make them do things differently in their lives. If video technology is available to you, record the performance and have the whole class review it. In this way, they will be able to assess their own work. They can discuss these matters as a whole group or write their responses in their drama books with words or pictures. Some teachers may want to record information from these assessments by using checklists or jotting down anecdotal notes.

Although these methods may not seem formal, they are still valid, because "informal measures are generally based on student work samples and student interactions during naturally occurring classroom situations" (Peregoy & Boyle, 2008, p. 106). In this way, informal assessment can provide a more direct measure of student ability.

The type of assessment tools and methods you choose will depend on what you want to assess, which should be directly connected to how you wanted your students to benefit from the playmaking experience in the first place. In addition to the overall learning objectives of playmaking, do you have any other more specific goals for this project? What are you most interested in finding out about your students? What type of information would be the most helpful in informing your instruction? In what specific areas do you want your students to grow? You should consider all these matters before you embark on a playmaking project. Inevitably, your students will have fun and show growth in a number of ways, but the following are just a few suggestions for how you might want to conduct assessment as students engage in playmaking activities.

Dramatic Performance

As stated previously, playmaking is not designed solely to produce master actors for stage and screen. However, the activities do provide different ways for children to demonstrate and develop their manner of artistic expression, as well as satisfy The National Standards for Arts Education in theatre - Content Standard #2, which involves students "Acting by assuming roles and interacting in improvisations." You may use the following criteria to help you observe different aspects of your students' performances.

Physical Characterization – Did the student use facial expression, movements, and gestures that were appropriate for the character? Were props, costumes, or scenery used in a way that was logical and relevant to the character?

Vocal Characterization – Was the actor's voice loud and clear? Did he or she use expression and tone appropriate for the character and the situation?

Internal Characterization – Overall, was the character portrayed believable? Was the actor able to stayed focused and "in character?" Did he or she act and react to other characters in a logical way?

Technical Knowledge of Play Production

Your students will acquire knowledge of the components of a play and how plays are executed throughout the playmaking process. Some ways to assess this understanding include observing how they interact and communicate with one another within the performance space and noting what they say during discussions about an enactment. Consider the extent to which your students use dramatic arts terminology when discussing dramatizations, set design, and developing improvisational situations. Are they able to name and describe the roles and responsibilities involved with a play or dramatic performance? Watch to see if they use creativity to choose and arrange various materials (from the prop box or brought from home) to design appropriate props, scenery, and costuming for dramatizations. You could also ask them to draw a picture of students engaged in dramatic performance and have them label different items, elements, or actions (such as actor, prop, scenery, audience, etc).

Character Analysis

This will be of great value as you help your students connect their playmaking experience to the literacy skills you are trying to reinforce. As your students talk with each other and respond to questions about characters after an enactment (whether performed by other students or by professional actors on a field trip to see a play), check to see if they can do the following:

♦ describe aspects of actors' performances (how they used their body and voice to convey the characters)
♦ compare and contrast a character's behaviors and personality with their own
♦ compare and contrast characters from the same enactment or other enactments
♦ identify a character's main traits and provide evidence from the dramatization to support this

- ◆ discuss how a character's traits or point of view might have changed in the course of the dramatization and why
- ◆ explain the reasons why they think a character reacts to situations in a certain way

Knowledge of Theme/Topic

When your class started the playmaking process, the first thing you did was help them choose a theme to explore. You may want to determine how well they have been able to internalize and understand the issues involved with that theme. Assess the extent to which your students were able to use the research from their readings, field trips, and personal experience to support classroom dramatizations. See if they can relate the dramatized situations to their own lives or connect them to other areas of study. Before the playmaking process begins, your class could fill out a K-W-L chart (Ogle, 1986), with one column for what they *know* about the theme and another for what they *want* to know. Reserve the last column for what your students have *learned* about the theme when the playmaking project is finished, and compare it to the other columns to see how their knowledge has changed. After each dramatization, you could pose a couple of questions about what they have learned by watching or participating in the performance. They could actually write or draw their responses in their drama books, too.

Language Arts Development and Connections

How you conduct your playmaking instruction can be greatly influenced by the information you gather from your regular language arts assessments. If you find that your students are having difficultly with some strategy or skill, you may be able to review, practice, or reinforce it through playmaking. Say, for example, that your last few writing assessments indicate some students have difficulty adding details to narratives to provide a sense of their characters' personality. Then after playmaking dramatizations, you may decide to ask those specific students questions about how actors could use or modify their performance skills to show particular character traits on stage. After some practice with this type of analysis, you could ask students to not only say their suggestions, but to try to write down those ideas on paper, describing things the actor should do or say to make their character's personality clear to the audience. This is a one way to transition children to analyzing and revising their own narratives by adding relevant character actions and phrases.

Conversely, playmaking gives your students relevant experiences and practice that you can help them reference during language arts lessons, guided reading groups, or in one-to-one conferences to illustrate your teaching points. If you are trying to teach your students about pre-writing before drafting or publishing their work, you can have them recall the "Create a Story" phase of the playmaking process, where they used a story map to help plan dramatizations. Similarly, they can use a story map (if they are writing a narrative) or some other graphic organizer to plan their writing. If you are trying to help your students make self-to-text connections to aid their reading comprehension, you could refer them to the times that they performed and brought characters to life by drawing from their own similar experiences.

Social/Emotional Growth

Collaboration is a key part of almost every aspect of the playmaking process, whether between children or a teacher and students. Therefore, you are likely to make assessments of whole groups of students just as much as individuals. Observe how students cooperate when planning and performing improvisations. See if they take turns and allow others to speak. Are students able to occasionally put their own wants on hold for the sake of the group? Are they able to share their opinions and preferences without disrespecting others? To what extent do they make an effort to make everyone feel included? How often do they help others who do not understand?

AFTERWORD

One of the most important things that I hope you take away from *The Playmaking Way* is that education through guided discovery can be so much more fulfilling for children than "chalk and talk," due to the feeling of accomplishment they get from knowing that they have played a significant role in making themselves smarter and forming their own meaning of the world around them. The type of active engagement described in *The Playmaking Way* can be a powerful tool in helping your students understand and retain the literacy concepts that you are trying to teach, or any other subject matter as well. The fact that you and your students just happen to be having fun in the process does not mean that real learning isn't still going on.

I also hope you have seen that the arts do not have to be on the fringe or dismissed as simply "extracurricular." On the contrary, playmaking actually makes drama more "co-curricular," because it develops a valuable set of critical thinking, social-emotional, and problem solving skills that are essential to children growing into happy, healthy, culturally competent human beings.

You have the power to change your students' lives. For that child that was once shy, and is now coming out of their shell. That child that is still learning English and was insecure about speaking, but has now found another mode of expression on stage. That advanced child that was once bored in class, but now has renewed enthusiasm for school because they are challenged and stimulated. That child that has a story inside them bursting to get out, real or imagined, painful or joyous, that finally has a forum to share it. Because you took the time to introduce them to playmaking, you have transformed potentially negative feelings about education, into positive. You have changed their perspective about what it means to go to school and learn. When children get a sense that you are willing to recognize and build off of the unique intelligence and prior knowledge that they all have, they come to school feeling that to be smart, accomplished, and successful is not only a possibility, but a near certainty that is within their grasp.

No matter what their age, ethnicity, or economic status, all children crave the opportunity to express themselves and be acknowledged for their talents, whatever those talents might be. When I think back on all the great teachers I have had, whether inside or outside of school, they all had a way of providing me with these types of opportunities.

Of course, keeping students engaged in this way is not always easy, especially the larger and more diverse the class. That is why I have offered this book to you. It is one practical way that I have discovered to bring beauty and enlightenment to the lives of my students, and to my life as an educator. I am confident that it will do the same for you. Enjoy!

REFERENCES

Case, R. (1998). The development of conceptual structures. In D. Kuhn & R. S. Siegler (Eds.) *Handbook of Child Psychology* (5th ed.), *Vol 2: Cognition, perception and language* (pp. 745–800). New York: Wiley.

Cole, M., Cole, S., & Lightfoot, C. (2005). *The development of children* (5th ed.). New York: Worth Publishers.

Cunningham, P. M., & Allington, R. L. (2007). *Classrooms that work: They all can read and write.* (4th ed.). Boston: Pearson.

Dewey, J. (1938). *Experience and education.* New York: Simon & Schuster.

Gallas, K. (1991). Arts as epistemology: Enabling children to know what they know. *Harvard Educational Review, 61*(1), 40.

Greene, M. (2001). *Variations on a blue guitar: The Lincoln Center Institute lectures on aesthetic education.* New York: Teachers College.

Kerman, G. (1961). *Plays and creative ways with children.* Irvington-on-Hudson: Harvey House Publishers.

Lukens, R. J. (2003). *A critical handbook of children's literature.* Boston: Allyn & Bacon.

McCaslin, N. (1997). *Creative drama in the primary grades: A handbook for teachers.* Studio City: Players Press.

Ogle, D. M. (1986). K-W-L: A teaching model that develops active reading of expository text. *The Reading Teacher, 39*(6), 564–570.

Peregoy, S. F., & Boyle, O. F. (2008). *Reading, writing and learning in ESL: A resource book for teaching K–12 english learners.* (5th ed.). Boston: Pearson.

Piaget, J. (1932/1965). *The Moral Judgment of the Child.* New York: Free Press.

Rasmussen, K. (1998). Arts education: A cornerstone of basic education. *Curriculum Update, Spring 1998,* 1–7.

Rockwell, R. E., Andre, L. C., & Hawley, K. (1996). *Parents and teachers as partners: Issues and challenges.* Fort Worth: Harcourt Brace.

Root-Bernstein, R. S. (1997). For the sake of science, the arts deserve support. *The Chronicle of Higher Education, 43*(44), B6.

Swap, S. (1993). *Developing home-school partnerships: From concepts to practice.* New York: Teachers College Press.

Wood, C. (2007). *Yardsticks: Children in the classroom ages 4–14: A resource for parents and teachers.* Greenfield: Northeast Foundation for Children.

APPENDICES

A. Classroom Diagram
B. Sample Pacing Calendar
C. Sample Thematic Bibliography
D. Sample Parent Participation Letter
E. Sample Drama Journals
F. Excerpt of Script
G. National Standards for Theatre

APPENDIX A: CLASSROOM DIAGRAM

The diagram on the following page is just one example of an early childhood classroom set-up. You may use the legend below to identify the various areas within it.

A. Math/Science Center

B. Playmaking Performance Area (*desks were sometimes moved back to make more space*)

C. Group/Meeting Area (*a "sight word" wall, calendar, and graphic organizers were posted here; this areas was also used a performance or practice space*)

D. Literacy Center (*includes Listening Center with audio equipment*)

E. Computer Center

F. Library

G. Art Center/Supplies

H. Desks/Audience (*on the day of the performance, these desks were moved into the Literacy Center, while the chairs remained to create seating for the audience*)

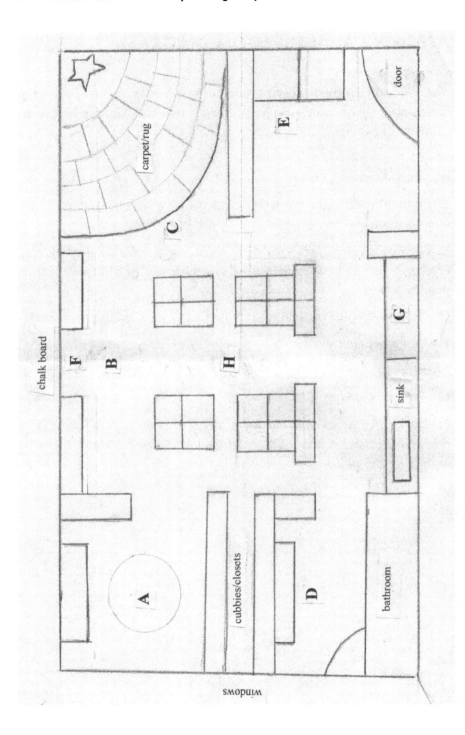

APPENDIX B: SAMPLE PACING CALENDAR

Below is a sample pacing calendar based on a six-week playmaking unit I conducted during the springtime. However, depending on the needs, desires, and learning objectives of your class, and how much time you allow for these activities, your students' playmaking project could be accomplished in as little as four weeks or stretched out as long as eight weeks. Note that due to the nature of playmaking, many of these activities can overlap. For example, much of the script developed while we "Explored the Theme" or were in the "Acting Out" phase. Therefore, any pacing calendar you create should act as a general framework with the assumption that some flexibility will be inherent in it.

WEEK	ACTIVITIES
1	**Explore a Theme:** Read-alouds, storytelling, journal writing, field trips, discussions, story mapping
2	**Explore a Theme** **Create Stories:** Small group work, presentations, and discussions of story maps **Acting Out:** Theatre games, pantomime, and improvisation
3	**Create Stories** **Acting Out** **Set Design, Props, Costuming:** Students create necessary scenery or items to use while acting
4	**Acting Out** **Set Design, Props, Costuming**
5	**Scripting/Casting:** Teacher transcribes student-created dialogue; students take on roles for the show **Rehearsal**
6	**Rehearsal** **Performance** **Follow-Up Activities**

APPENDIX C: SAMPLE THEMATIC BIBLIOGRAPHY –FAMILY

The following is an annotated bibliography of some of the books I used to explore the theme of "family" with first-grade students. Of course, the books you use will vary depending on the theme your class selects. Note that these titles are appropriate to share with kindergarten through third-grade children. They reflect cultural and socioeconomic diversity and span a variety of genres, including nonfiction, fantasy, folktale, and poetry.

Dorros, Arthur. 1991. *Abuela*. New York: Puffin Books
> The magical tale of an urban Latina child who explores her neighborhood by flying through the air with her *abuela* (grandmother in Spanish). Spanish language words are interjected and explained within the English-language text.

Dorros, Arthur. 1992. *This is my house*. New York: Scholastic
> This picture book explores the similarities and differences between types of housing from all over the world. A variety of different structures and living situations are represented, including a family living out of their car.

Hoebermann, Mary Ann. 1991. *Fathers, mothers, sisters, brothers: A collection of family poems*. New York: Puffin Books
> This collection of 26 humorous poems explores characteristics of a variety of family members and relationships. It also explores growing up, shyness, having to eat dinner food you don't like, and wanting to be by yourself sometimes. It is best for read-alouds/sing-alouds.

Saunders-Smith, Gail. 1998. *Families*. Mankato: Capstone Press.
This nonfiction book describes the relationships among members of culturally diverse families. Each page has no more than one simple sentence and an accompanying photo. There is a glossary, bibliography, and web-bibliography.

Simon, Norma. 1976. *All kinds of families*. Morton Grove: Albert Whitman & Company.
This hardcover picture book uses both words and pictures to explore what a family is and how families vary in composition, lifestyles, ethnicity, size, age, and responsibilities. Due to its length, this book is best shared as a read-aloud.

Steptoe, John. 1987. *Mufaro's beautiful daughters: An African tale*. New York: Lothrop, Lee & Shepard Books
In this Caldecott Award–winning book, Steptoe creates a modern fable based on the classic Cinderella story. This version is set in an African village and features a mean sister, yet kind father. Due to its length, this is best shared as a read aloud.

APPENDIX D: SAMPLE PARENT PARTICIPATION LETTER

The following "Parent Participation Letter" can be modified to suit your needs. You may share it with parents at the beginning of the school year, just before the times that you want to start specific playmaking projects, or during a prearranged parent/teacher meeting or conference. If you, a staff person at your school, community center, local university or religious institution can write in the home language(s) of your English language learners, then you may also try to print a translation on the other side of the letter.

PARENT PARTICIPATION LETTER

Your Name: _____ Phone Number: _____ Your Child's Name: _____

Our class is doing dramatic arts in the classroom and we would like your support. Whatever time you can give would be greatly appreciated. You will get to help your child learn and have fun at the same time. Thank you for your cooperation!

Please put a check by what you would prefer to do or help with in the classroom, or any special talent you can share:

Reading to the class _____   Be interviewed/share stories (about your culture, life, job, or hobby) _____

Art (painting, drawing, sculpture) _____   Crafts (knitting, origami, woodwork, etc.) _____

Musical Instrument (guitar, piano, drums, horn, etc) _____   Singing _____   Dance _____

Storytelling _____   Video Taping _____   Other (please specify) _____

You may also let us know any specific dates or times that you might be available (example: Wednesday, October 24):

_____

_____

I can't come to the class, but I can send or lend the following:

Music/CDs _____   CD or tape player _____   Household items _____   Clothes/costumes _____

Video Camera _____   Snacks _____   Other (please specify) _____

APPENDIX E: SAMPLE DRAMA JOURNALS

The following pages are from the drama journals of first-grade students. Their class explored the theme of family conflict.

Figure 1.

This page was created as the student explored the theme. I prompted students by asking "What do families do together?" or "What do you like to do with your family?" However, they were free to write or draw pictures about any aspect of the theme.

Figure 2.

In figure 2 (above), another student shares a personal story involving family conflict. They rely heavily on drawings and make use of "balloons" to convey dialogue.

In figure 3 (opposite page), the writer relies less on pictures and more on words and sentences to convey their story. Their following page is from another day in class when we discussed the concept of a "script." Students were encouraged to reflect on what they had learned and write down things that were the most interesting to them or that they wanted to remember.

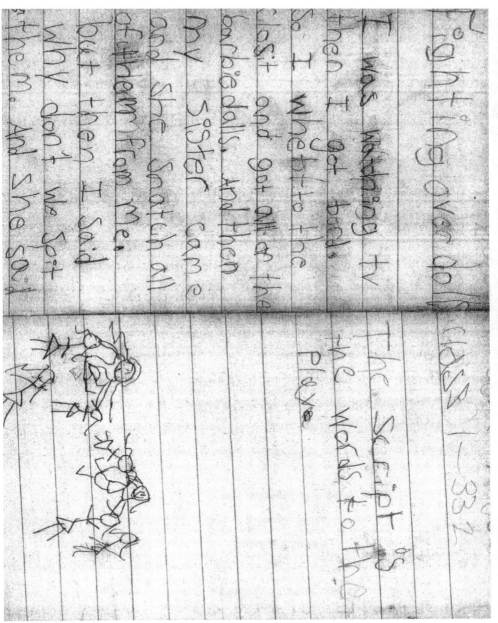

Fighting over dolls class 1-332

I was watching tv
then I got bad.
So I when to the
closit and got all of the
barbie dolls, And then
my sister came
and she snatch all
of them from me.
but then I said
why don't we spit
them. And she said

The script is
the words to the
playe

Figure 3.

APPENDIX F: EXCERPT OF SCRIPT

FAMILY DRAMA
A play written and performed by class 1-332
Directed by Ms. Rabin Nickens

Introductions: Good morning [principal and assistant principal], parents, teachers, students, and friends. Welcome to class 1-332. We are proud to present *Family Drama*, a play written by all of us. We hope you enjoy our show.

Act I: The Stroller Story

Setting: Amanda's bedroom, Saturday morning.

Narrator: Act I, The Stroller Story. One morning, Amanda woke up from a good night's sleep.

Amanda: (She yawns loudly and stretches her arms wide as she sits up in bed. She then looks around the room for something to play with.) Hmmm … what should I play with today? (Amanda gets out of bed and walks over to her toy box.)

Narrator: Amanda has so many toys to choose from.

Amanda: Should I pick this one?......No....Should I pick this one?......Uh, uh....Maybe I'll try my toy stroller. (She takes out the stroller and starts to play with it.) This is really fun!

Narrator: Just then, Amanda's baby sister knocked on the door.

(Knocking sound at the door.)

Amanda: Who is it?

Katey: It's me, Katey. Can I come in? I'm bored.

Amanda: Well … okay, but only for a little while.

Katey: Ooh … a toy stroller! Can I play?

Amanda: No!

Katey: Why not?

Amanda: Because I was playing with it first.

Katey: So? You have to share.

Amanda: No I don't!

Katey: Yes you do! Gimme! (Katey tries to snatch the stroller from Amanda and they begin a "tug-of-war" over it.)

Narrator: They fought and fought and fought. Amanda grabbed the stroller. Then Katey grabbed the stroller. (Amanda and Katey argue loudly, saying "yes" and "no"). They were so loud that they woke up their mother.

Mother: (She rushes into the bedroom.) What are you doing? What's going on?

Amanda: She took my stroller!

Katey: No, it's mine!

Mother: Stop it! (She says to Katey) Go to your room.

Katey: Why?

Mother: So you won't bother her anymore.

Katey: I wasn't.

Mother: So then why were you fighting her in the first place?

Katey: Because that was my stroller.

Amanda: No it wasn't!

Katey: Yes it was!

Mother: Stop fighting! See, you're doing it again! Go to your room!

Katey: Why doesn't she have to go to bed?

Mother: Because she's older.

(Katey stomps away angrily. Amanda smiles and teases her.)

Amanda: Aha!

Mother: You can't play with the stroller either. Go watch TV! (Amanda plops down on her bed sadly.) I'm going to take this and keep it in my room.

Narrators: And nobody got to play with the toy. The end.

Actors come out and change the set to "Act II: The Game Trouble."

APPENDIX G: NATIONAL STANDARDS FOR THEATRE (K-4)

The methods described in *The Playmaking Way* align with several of the National Standards for Arts Education, Theatre (K–4). For more information, including specific achievement standards for each content area, you may visit the Kennedy Center's ArtsEdge Web site (http://artsedge.kennedy-center.org/teach/standards. cfm), which states the following:

"Developed by the Consortium of National Arts Education Associations (under the guidance of the National Committee for Standards in the Arts), the National Standards for Arts Education is a document which outlines basic arts learning outcomes integral to the comprehensive K-12 education of every American student. The Consortium published the National Standards in 1994 through a grant administered by MENC, the National Association for Music Education."

Content Standard #1: Script writing by planning and recording improvisations based on personal experience and heritage, imagination, literature, and history

Content Standard #2: Acting by assuming roles and interacting in improvisations

Content Standard #3: Designing by visualizing and arranging environments for classroom dramatizations

Content Standard #4: Directing by planning classroom dramatizations

Content Standard #5: Researching by finding information to support classroom dramatizations

Content Standard #6: Comparing and connecting art forms by describing theatre, dramatic media (such as film, television, and electronic media), and other art forms

Content Standard #7: Analyzing and explaining personal preferences and constructing meanings from classroom dramatizations and from theatre, film, television, and electronic media productions

Content Standard #8: Understanding context by recognizing the role of theatre, film, television, and electronic media in daily life

GLOSSARY

This glossary of basic theatre terms can be used for your own reference or to help explain playmaking terminology to your students. Depending on the grade level and which phase of the playmaking process your students are in, you may also want to post some of these terms on a "Drama Word Wall."

active audience – students whose job is to think while observing an enactment or show and provide constructive feedback to the performers.

acts – the separate and distinct parts of a play. Acts often begin or end with the passage of time (ex: Act 1 ends at night, while Act 2 takes place the next morning). Similar to "chapters" in a book.

audience – the people who watch the show; the space in a theatre or auditorium designated for people to sit and watch a show.

auditorium – another term for "theatre." Often used in reference to a large performance space in a school.

backstage –the part of the stage where actors do not perform and cannot be seen. This is often behind a curtain, or sometimes in a room or hallway adjacent to the stage.

blocking – deciding where the actors should stand, sit, or move on stage during a performance.

center stage – the middle part of the stage. Halfway between downstage and upstage.

character – a person who is enacted in a play or other type of performance; who a play or story is mainly about.

costumes – the clothes and accessories an actor wears on stage to portray a character.

cue – a signal that tells the actor do something. It can be something seen (visual cue) or heard (audio cue).

dialogue – the words that two or more characters say to each other in a performance.

downstage – the area on stage closest to the audience; the area near the front edge of the stage.

drama book – a journal where students can write drama-related or theme-related entries.

improvisation – a performance where the words and actions are created spontaneously with little or no preparation; when actors create words and actions to convey a story or situation as they go along.

lines – the words an actor says in a performance; sentences in a script that show what an actor is supposed to say in a performance.

monologue – a speech said by one actor in a performance.

pantomime – a silent performance where an actor uses movements and gestures to convey the story, environment, and objects.

play – a show or performance; a story created to be performed for a live audience.

playmaking area – an area of the classroom cleared out and designated for dramatic performance; a mock stage in the classroom.

props – the materials or items an actor handles on stage to help convey a character and his or her habits; specifically "hand props."

run-through – the practice of a play or performance from beginning to end without stopping, as it would be done on the day of the show for an audience.

scene – a short story or situation that is performed; a small section of a play that takes place without change in time or place.

scenery – the background or furnishings on stage to represent a particular setting.

script – the written words of a play; a document that shows what the actors are supposed to say and do during a performance.

set – the stage prepared to look like a particular place or setting of a story or play; specific scenery is typically used on a set.

setting – the time and place where a story or play happens.

skit – a short or informal performance.

stage – a specific area designated for people to perform for an audience; usually on a raised platform in a theatre or auditorium.

stage directions – the instructions on where the actors should go or how they should move.

story map – a graphic organizer that shows the different elements of a story.

theme – the main topic or subject of a story or play.

upstage – the area on stage farthest back from the audience.

INDEX

NOTES

PLAYMAKING ORDER FORM

Please send me _____ **copies of** *The Playmaking Way: Using Dramatic Arts to Support Young Readers and Writers.*

Please send me more FREE information on:

__ Speaking/Seminars   __ Consulting   __ Other Books

(You may also send inquiries to RabinNickens@gmail.com)

Name: _____

Addres: _____

City: _____   **State:** _____   **Zip:** _____

Telephone: _____

Email Address: _____

Retail Price: $21.95 (plus shipping)

Shipping: $5 shipping for first book and $3 for each additional book in the U.S. (Estimated International Shipping: $10 for first book and $5 for each additional book)

Please mail order form with certified check or money order to:

Third Power Publishing
P.O. Box 715
New York, NY 10037
U.S.A.